ORIENTAL EXPRESS

Chinese Menus for the Food Processor

by Barbara Grunes

introduction by Maxine Horowitz

Cover Design by Stanley Drate
Illustrations by Betty Acosta
Art Director Tom Nova
Photos by Nick Ruscio

Good Food Books

TABLE OF CONTENTS

INTRODUCTION

With due respect to the cleaver and the Chinese grandmother, the ancient Oriental techniques of shredding, chopping, grating, grinding, and mincing required by Oriental cookery are no match for the convenience of the food processor. The design of this book is to help you simplify the preparation of this exciting and varied cuisine so that long tedious hours in the kitchen become shorter and Chinese cooking becomes synonomous with relaxed dining for you and your guests.

Barbara has been cooking Chinese food for many years and teaching it for the past seven. Her mentor and first teacher was Madame Mai Leung from whom she learned the high style of Oriental cuisine. From her experience in cooking for students, friends, and family, she has collected the most popular of her recipes, and adapted them to machine cookery for the American palate.

Maxine is best known for her first book, "Inside the Food Processor", which enjoyed national success for its simple, straight forward approach to cooking with the food processor In the New York area, where she lives, her classes are a must for anyone who's not quite sure what to do once she's got the processor out of the box.

The authors have collaborated to bring you the best of both their skills. This little book will take you with ease from the picnic grounds to the banquet setting—a full range of meal options are included. Everything here begins and ends with the finest, freshest ingredients. It's all made fast and easy by the food processor. The food combinations are compatible, but not immutable. For example, the Chinese traditionally serve several categories of food—fish, soup, vegetables—at one meal. With a low bow to local custom, we have included dessert.

Plan your meal, assemble your components, ready your machine, and then enjoy!

THOUGHTS FROM A CHINESE-AMERICAN KITCHEN....

Most Chinese recipes are prepared in a wok, which is a very efficient cooking utensil. While stir-frying, it provides a large heated surface to cook the food quickly, and in deep frying it provides the largest amount of cooking surface with the least amount of oil. A heavy frying pan may be used in many recipes. An electric fryer may be substituted when deep frying.

1

Season the wok before it is used for the first time. Wash the wok thoroughly with hot sudsy water, rinse and wipe dry. Add 2 tablespoons of vegetable oil. Heat for 30 seconds and carefully tilt and rotate the wok until the entire inner surface is coated with the oil. Wipe the wok with paper towels until the complete inner surface is smooth and only a thin coating of oil remains.

Many recipes in this book begin with 3 to 5 tablespoons of peanut oil. The wok should always be hot before the oil is added. It is important to maintain a high heat for the entire cooking process unless otherwise noted.

Stir-frying is the Chinese cooking technique used most often in our recipes. First the ingredients are prepared and placed near the wok. Meat and vegetables are cut into small pieces so they will cook quickly. The wok is heated until it is smoking, a little oil is added, and then the ingredients (according to each recipe's directions) are added and stirred constantly during the cooking by moving and turning them in the hot wok. The cooking time is just a few minutes, and the results are crisp and succulent. With a little practice, you will be able to master this distinctive cooking technique.

Most recipes in this book serve from 4 to 6 people unless otherwise stated. The number of servings varies according to how many other dishes are being served at the same meal. Don't add to much food to the wok at one time as it lowers the temperature of the wok, making it impossible to cook quickly at a high heat. For larger quantities, prepare a recipe twice in sequence.

Remember to assemble all of the ingredients near the stove in the order in which they are to be added to the work. Prepare ingredients for several dishes before starting to cook, and then the actual cooking time is very short. Don't attempt to prepare more than 2 or 3 different dishes for one meal while you are a "beginner." When using the processor several times in one recipe, it will not be necessary to wash the bowl in between different processes.

On the banquet table, each person should have a bowl of rice, a bowl for soup, a plate for the main course and a small dish for sauces, a soup spoon and a pair of chopsticks. For a simple meal a single bowl and a pair of chopsticks is enough. The Oriental style is to serve one dish at a time, accompanied by rice or noodles. The traditional Chinese way to serve soup is after the entrees have been offered, but before the dessert.

Arrange the food attractively on serving platters or in bowls. Careful attention to appearance is very important in the presentation of Chinese food; it should be pleasing to the eye and have an appealing aroma.

There are very few traditional Chinese desserts. Fruit is usually served at the end of a meal. However, in deference to our own American taste, we have included some recipes for other simple desserts that will be suitable to use with a Chinese meal.

To use chopsticks for eating, place one chopstick in the right hand, held by the base of the thumb and the top of the middle and index finger. The first (lower) chopstick remains stationary while the second one is moved up and down by the middle and index finger. (You will be holding it like a pencil.) The thumb remains in an almost unchanged position. Practice!

The temperature for deep frying is 375 degrees as used in this book. The Chinese way is to take a wooden chopstick and place the end in the oil. If bubbles form around the chopsticks, then the oil is ready for deep frying. The chopstick is a great cooking tool—try one.

You can improvise a steamer by adding a perforated rack to your dutch oven or extra wok.

The cleaver is an important tool in the Chinese kitchen, but the food processor has made a cleaver almost unnecessary. It is so much faster and easier to do your slicing and chopping in your processor!

SPECIAL CHINESE INGREDIENTS

Remember that it is worth the extra effort to get authentic ingredients. In large metropolitan areas, this is no problem as most things are available in supermarkets now, and there are many Oriental specialty shops as well. Cooks from rural areas may have to take more trouble to obtain what they need. One shopping trip can fill your needs for a long time for things that can be stored, such as soy sauce, oyster sauce, ginger root, water chestnuts, black beans, hoisin sauce, Chinese dried mushrooms, and sesame oil. Substitutions can be made if necessary for Chinese produce. For example, if you can't obtain fresh peapods (snow peas), use thinly sliced green peppers— they will add the proper crunchiness and color and the result will be much better than if you used frozen peapods.

When a recipe calls for sesame oil, be sure to use the Chinese sesame oil, not the health food variety. Sesame oil is a strong and pungent oil with a nutlike flavor. It is not used for frying, but for flavor. A teaspoonful poured on top of any dish will enhance its flavor.

3

Vermicelli or fun-see are sold in long packages. There are two types of vermicelli, those made from mung bean flour, and the rice noodles made from rice flour. Both are semi-translucent and brittle. Fun-see can be stir-fried, steamed or deep fried. When it is deep fried it puffs up into a white bird's nest shape. It must be presoaked for stir-fry or steamed dishes.

Fresh ginger always adds the best flavor and is important to have. If it is not available, substitute 1/4 teaspoon ground ginger for one slice of fresh ginger. One slice of ginger in the recipes in this book always means a slice that is the size of a quarter. Ginger can be stored in the refrigerator or in a jar covered with sherry or sterile sand. (Sterile sand can usually be purchased at a hardware store.) It will also keep for two weeks or so uncovered at room temperature.

Flank steak is an excellent meat to use for stir-frying. Be sure to cut it against the grain. If you don't use flank steak, you can substitute sirloin, round, or chuck steak.

Good soup starts with a good strong broth. Always use either chicken or a combination of chicken and pork for the basic stock. Beef has too strong and hearty a flavor for Chinese dishes. Canned chicken broth is good too.

Dried mushrooms are used in many of these recipes. If they are not available, you may use fresh mushrooms, though there is a difference in the taste.

Bean curd is a soft custard-like paste made from soy beans. Bean curd, or "tofu" as it is also called, can be obtained at health food stores, Chinese food stores, and some super-markets. It should be kept refrigerated in a bowl of water and the water should be changed every day.

When wine is in a recipe, you may use sherry, dry white wine, rice wine, or sake.

Tabasco may be used instead of red pepper.

Both the black and white variety of sesame seeds may be used. For added flavor they may be toasted, but they burn easily and need to be watched carefully.

Black beans are a small and salty bean and are used to season meat and fish. They should be washed first, then minced with the fresh garlic and ginger in the recipe. Black beans can be stored at room temperature.

Green vegetables will have a brighter and fresher color if a little salt is first sprinkled in the oil.

Tea was originally packed in solid cakes. One would chip away at it, crush it, mix it with orange peel and then boil it. Tea still remains the most popular drink in China. There are numerous varieties of Chinese tea. Be adventuresome and experiment. Try a delicate floral or black or green tea.

Hoisin sauce is obtainable in cans in Chinese groceries and some supermarkets. It is used in dips as well as seasoning and sauces. Once opened, it can be stored in the refrigerator in tightly covered jars.

The 2 kinds of soy sauce are thick and thin, sometimes called dark and light. Thin or light soy sauce is saltier and heavy soy is used more for color and pungency. Soy sauces keep well at room temperature if tightly capped.

Oyster sauce imparts a smooth velvety texture and a rich flavor to sauces. It should be stored in the refrigerator.

If you have a vegetable garden, try growing some Chinese vegetables. Nothing could be better! The important thing is to use the best ingredients that you can, but if some special ones are not available, don't be discouraged, cook anyway. The flavor may be a little different, but it will still be good!

ALL ABOUT BEAN SPROUTS

It is better to use fresh bean sprouts than canned ones. Try sprouting your own.

To sprout mung beans, soak 1/2 cup of mung beans overnight in warm water. They should double in size. Wet triple folds of paper towels and place on the bottom of a cookie sheet. Place beans on towel. Wet another triple fold of paper towels and cover the beans. Leave them in a warm place (70-75 degrees) such as the inside of your oven or the top of your refrigerator.

Rinse mung beans every morning and night, then return to the cookie sheet. The sprouts are ready to use when they are 1½-2½ inches tall. Check them on the third day. Place in a bowl of cold water, and swish sprouts around to separate them from any remaining seed coats, which will drop to the bottom or float off. Finally, the sprouts are ready to enjoy. They will keep for several days in the refrigerator in a plastic bag.

HOW TO COOK RICE

Rice should always be well washed before cooking to remove the talc which coats it. Use long grained rice. To cook rice, you should use a heavy pot with a tight-fitting cover. Start the rice in cold water and with heat high. When the water comes to the boiling point, reduce the heat to low, cover the rice, and steam for about 15 minutes. Remove the pan from the heat and let it stand covered for 10 to 15 minutes.

5

To warm up left-over rice, add 1 teaspoon cold water to each cup of cold cooked rice. Loosen the grains with a fork, then heat slowly over a slow fire for 8 to 10 minutes. Cover tightly and let the steam cook the rice until it is hot.

If you wish to be adventurous you might try growing your own Chinese vegetables from seeds. Sixteen varieties are available, each selling for $.69 each plus postage and handling.

Also available is a set of five regional Oriental spices in shaker bottles that can be used as the base for appetizer dips as well as being the flavor base for all kinds of cooking from the numerous provences of China. These spices will really help you "Express" yourself in your Oriental cooking.

For more information and price lists, send a self addressed stamped envelope to:

Good Food Books
17 Colonial Terrace
Maplewood, N.J. 07040

Chinese ingredients not available in your area can be ordered by mail from:

Oriental Food Market
7411 North Clark St.
Chicago, Il. 60626

THE PROCESSOR

Before you begin cooking it is most important to familiarize yourself with the parts of the machine and their functions. The following pages of this book are the key to your success with your processor, so take a few moments to read them over carefully. *If you have never been to a demonstration or class, it is even more crucial that you read these pages.*

PARTS OF THE MACHINE

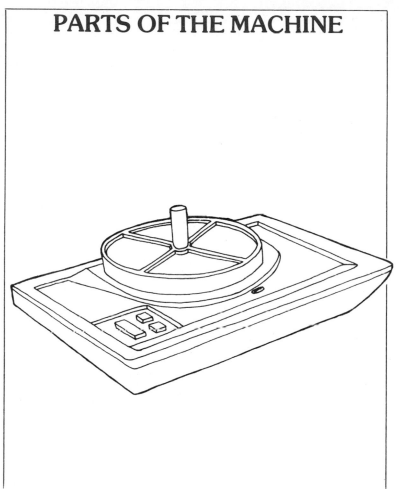

A. **Motor Base.** The steel or *Lexan* ® housed motor base is the source of power for your food processor. All machines, whether direct drive (as are the ones shown in this book) or belt driven, are equipped with a drive shaft extending from the center of the base. You will notice that all the machines have an indented dot on the front of the base. In many cases this dot becomes your ON/OFF switch. In some of the more recent or "second generation" machines there is an actual switch to activate the motor. These newer machines also have a "PULSE" or "FLASH" switch which enables you to rapidly turn the machine on and off to chop, a technique done with a twist of the wrist in the "1st generation" machines.

The motor on the food processor is sealed so you need not worry about shocks. It is not immersible and thus should only be wiped down with warm soapy water.

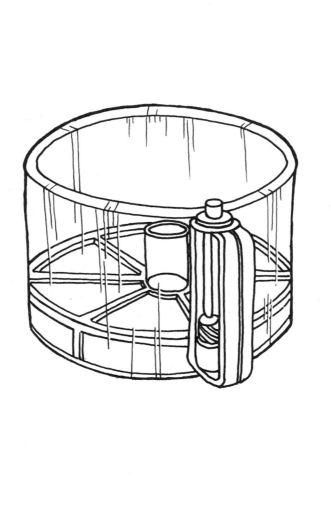

B. **Workbowl.** The workbowl, with or without handle is made of Lexan® , a shatterproof plastic that is used for airplane windows. On the side of the bowl you will notice a stem protruding. This contains a spring action which when in place over the dot on the front of the base, will activate the motor. In the case of machines with manual switches placement of the bowl will prepare the machine to be started.

    The bowl, as well as the cover, blades and spatula are dishwasher proof. It is preferable to wash these parts by hand using a soft sponge or brush. You may air or towel dry these parts.

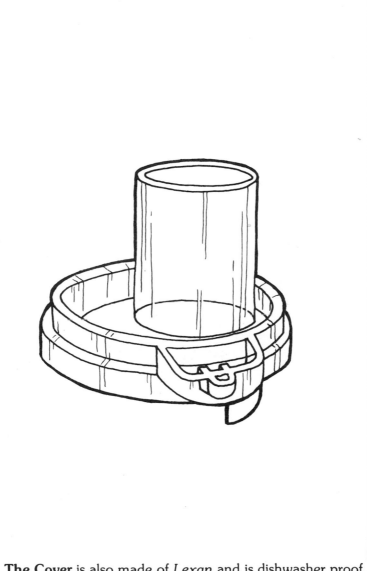

C. **The Cover** is also made of *Lexan* and is dishwasher proof. Protruding from the top is the *feed tube* where much food is processed and the only way to add ingredients while the machine is in operation. On the edge of the cover, just below and to the left of the feed tube you will find a small extension. If you own a machine without external switches this piece must be pushed in place over the stem of the bowl to engage the motor. This same method is used when machines are equipped with manual switches. Once the bowl and lid are completely in place the switch will start the motor.

D. **The Pusher** is used to guide food through the feed tube into the slicing or shredding disks. *It is not dishwasher safe.* This piece should also be used when processing liquids or flour in order to eliminate splashback. *Always use the pusher, never your fingers to push food through the feed tube.* The design of each pusher is slightly different. Some have open tops, others are closed. Several with open tops are calibrated so that you can use them as a one cup measure.

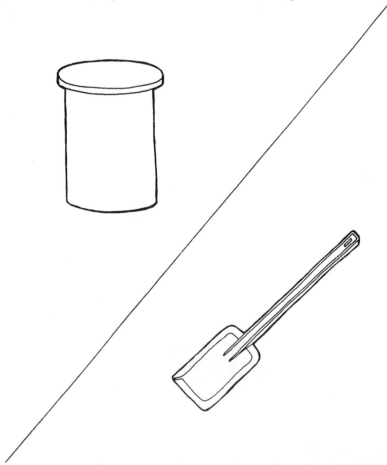

E. **The Spatula** is used to scrape food from the sides of the workbowl. The firm plastic construction enables you to clean out the bowl with little effort. *Never try to use the spatula while the food process is operating.*

These are the basic parts of the machine. Before a description of each blade and its function is presented it is important to have an explanation of the principles of operation.

OPERATION

The machine should be plugged into a 120 volt electrical outlet and placed on a firm surface. Be sure to use a properly grounded outlet, unless the cord is double insulated. You should stand your machine in a convenient place on the counter, (always store it unplugged) with the front facing you. Place the workbowl over the drive shaft with the vertical stem just slightly to the left of the indented dot, or the line on the base. Push the bowl into place over the dot with your hands. *If the bowl is not exactly in place the machine will not start.* Each machine has a slightly different method for locking the bowl into place. If you see that the method suggested here does not work with your machine then refer to your owner's manual. Place one of the blades or disks in place over the drive shaft and spin it slowly with your fingertips until it slips down and locks in place.

If your machine is equipped with a pulse switch you will PULSE wherever you see a reference to on/off. The pulse replaces a manual turn of the wrist. Machines vary in the length of the pulse so you will have to experiment with different types of foods until you get the desired results.

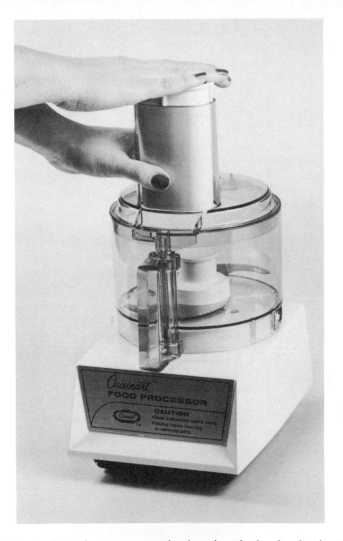

Next, place the cover on the bowl with the feed tube just to the left of the vertical stem. Place your hand on the side of the feed tube and turn the entire cover to the right, pulling the plastic lip extending below the rim of the lid into place over the vertical stem. This will push the spring down. When the spring is depressed it activates the motor. In order to stop the machine you must move the lid to the left, out of place, and allow the spring to be released.

If your machine has the on/off switch, the lid must be securely in place before the switch will go on. (The lid should never be removed while blade is spinning). This is the off position. *Your machine should always be stored in the off position.*

BLADES AND THEIR USES

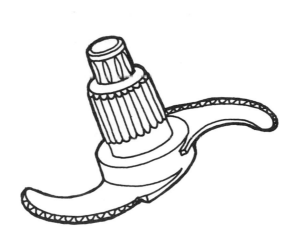

Steel Blade

The double sided steel blade is your most versatile tool. It will do the function of a blender, mixer, and meat grinder. Hard foods or ice cubes should be added through the feed tube which you can over cover with your hand between additions.

There are times when the processing will be very loud. As the pieces get chopped the noise decreases. If the machine starts to move on the counter, place your hand on the base, and again, as the pieces become smaller, the movement will stop. Do not put more than 2 cups of food in the workbowl to be chopped with this blade as it may create uneven results.

There are several techniques that must be learned in order to operate the machine in a satisfactory manner. The first is the ON/OFF method. This refers to a quick wrist motion which turns the machine on, then off immediately. This method gives you control of results. The processor works so quickly that you must check the bowl after one or two on/off turns, particularly if you are chopping soft foods like mushrooms or onions.

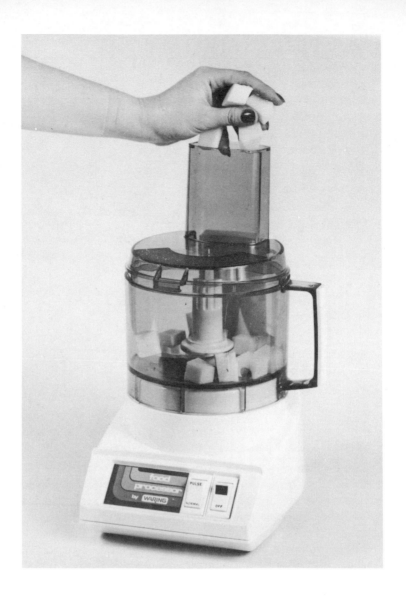

The second technique is to let the machine run to mix, knead dough, puree, or process foods which need time, such as mayonnaise or peanut butter.

The third technique is dropping food through the feed tube while the machine is operating. This technique is used for mincing small quantities of food such as 1 or 2 cloves of garlic, for crushing ice, or grating hard cheeses like parmesan. In addition, you may add food to a recipe already being processed in the workbowl, i.e. adding eggs or flour to cake batter.

To chop firm vegetables (potatoes, carrots, turnips)

Cut the food into pieces no larger than 1-1/2" on a side. Place up to 2 cups of cubes into the workbowl with the blade in place. Turn the machine on and off quickly several times using the feed tube as a handle. Check to see if the pieces are the desired size. Continue turning the machine on and off until the pieces are the required size. *This is most important for controlling the size and texture of the food you are processing.* Using this method also allows pieces of food which have been thrown up the sides of the bowl, to drop down close to the blade and be processed.

To chop soft vegetables (onions, scallions, peppers)

Be sure onions are halved or quartered and other vegetables are in chunks no large than 1-1/2"-2". Use a very fast on/off turn once or twice and then check. Soft vegetables process quickly and if you let the machine run you will extract the juices. If the vegetables are processed properly there should be a minimum of juice in the bowl.

To chop parsley or other herbs

Be sure the blade and bowl are dry. Put a large or small amount of greens in the bowl, with or without stems, and process using the on/off method. Store in a closed container in the refrigerator.

To chop raw meat

Cut cold or partially frozen meat into 1" cubes and remove loose fat and gristle. Place up to 1/4 lb. of cubes into the workbowl and using the on/off method chop until the desired fineness is achieved. Remove cover to check texture. If you find the meat catching on the blade, turn the machine on and drop the meat, all at once, through the feed tube and continue to process as directed above.

To chop cooked meat

Follow the same procedure as for raw meat. You may chop other ingredients with the meat such as vegetables, herbs, bread crumbs or eggs.

To grate parmesan cheese

In order to get a fine texture, many people like to process this cheese with the steel blade rather than with the grating disk. Be sure that the parmesan or any hard cheese is at room temperature and cut it into 1/2" pieces. Start the machine and add the cubes through the feed tube. Turn on and off several times, then let the machine run until the cheese is finely grated.

To make peanut or other nut butters

Be certain that the blades are covered with nuts. Turn the machine on and off then let the machine run until a paste forms on the side of the bowl. You may want to add a small amount of oil or butter at this time to improve the spreading consistency.

To chop and grind nuts

Place nuts in workbowl and use the on/off method until the nuts are chopped to the desired fineness. A coarse chop will only take a few turns. If you want to grind nuts for a torte, add a small amount of flour from the recipe, and continue to process, checking the bowl every few seconds. DO NOT over process or you will have a nut butter.

To make bread crumbs or cracker crumbs

You may use fresh or stale bread, broken up. French bread should be in smaller pieces as it takes longer to process. Crackers should also be broken up. Use the on/off method until desired texture is achieved.

To beat egg whites

Be sure that the workbowl and blade are clean, dry, and free of grease. Place at least 4 egg whites in the bowl with 1/4 tsp. salt or cream of tartar. Process until the desired stiffness is achieved. Remove whites from the workbowl and gently place in a mixing bowl. Do not try to fold ingredients into the whites in the workbowl or you will lose the volume. You will notice that you have a reduced volume using the food processor for this process. When maximum volume is necessary use an electric mixer.

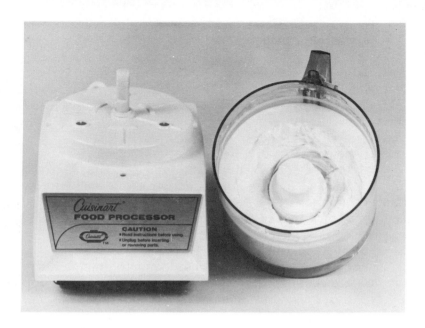

To whip cream

Chill the bowl and blade for 15 minutes. Pour the cold cream into the workbowl. Put the pusher in place and turn the machine on. Remove the pusher to let the air in. After about a minute, or when the cream has thickened to the consistency of sour cream, you can add flavoring through the feed tube. Continue to process until the cream has begun to form a rim on the side of the bowl. You may stop the machine to check. Look through the feed tube; if there is any liquid remaining on the bottom, continue to process. *Don't leave the machine running or you may get butter.* This cream will be heavy and stiff, but will be adequate for toppings.

To make pastry dough

Place dry ingredients in the workbowl with cold shortening or frozen butter that has been cup up. Insert pusher. Turn machine on and off several times to cut the butter to the desired fineness. With the machine running, add liquid through the feed tube. Process only until you see the dough starting to form a ball over the blade. Even if all the dough is not in a ball, stop the machine, and press the loose pieces into the larger mass by hand. *Do not over process or the dough will be tough.* Chill or roll out. Use your favorite recipe, but best results are achieved using no more than 1-1/2 cups of flour at a time. The machine works so quickly you can repeat the operation for a larger quantity, rather than overloading it the first time.

Mixing cakes

It is possible to mix cakes in the food processor. You must bear in mind that the blade does not aerate like a mixer, therefore, light textured cakes are best not done with the machine. Quick breads, other cakes that do not require prolonged beating, or cakes which require separate beating of yolks and whites can be made successfully. It is important to remember that when baking soda is used you must not overprocess or you will get a tough cake.

To make flavored spreads or butters

Place solid ingredients to be chopped in the workbowl. Process using the on/off method until food is finely chopped. Add butter or cheeses and process until smooth. If liquids are to be added, cut down on the quantity until you check the texture of the mixture.

Slicing Disk

The **slicing disk** will slice vegetables, cheese, and frozen meat. The basic technique for control with this disk is the amount of pressure exerted on the pusher while the food is being sliced. The heavier the pressure, the thicker the slice. The lighter the pressure, the thinner the slice. It is also important that the food being sliced is wedged firmly in place. If the food is allowed to move freely in the feed tube it will be sliced on an angle and the pieces will not be uniform.

On certain processors, the bottom of the feed tube is slightly wider than the top, so that food that is slightly too large to fit in through the top may be wedged in from the bottom.

To slice round thin vegetables (carrots, celery)

Cut the vegetables in lengths just a little shorter than the feed tube. Be sure that the tops and bottoms are cut straight across. Wedge the pieces in firmly. If you are only slicing one or two stalks of celery, cut the pieces shorter but a uniform length, and wedge in place, insert the pusher and exert the appropriate pressure.

To slice round wide vegetables (zucchini, cucumber)

When you are shopping, learn to select thin vegetables that will wedge more easily into the feed tube. If they are unavailable you may have to trim the sides to fit them in. Again, be sure that the tops and bottoms are cut straight across. A 2" length will insure that the food does not have an opportunity to slip out of place while being sliced.

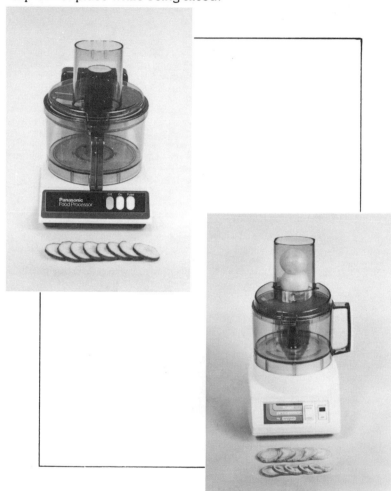

To slice onions

To make onion rings, cut the top and bottom off the onion and wedge in place or push to the right side of the feed tube. Exert firm pressure.

If your onion is too large to go in that way, lay it on its side and slice. If necessary, cut the onion in half lengthwise and wedge the pieces in upright. Exert firm pressure.

To slice soft fruits and vegetables (mushrooms, strawberries)

Hull berries and remove stems from mushrooms. Fill the feed tube and exert firm pressure. This procedure is used when you have large quantities to process. If you want perfect cross section slices, stand the berries on the blade, hull side down, replace cover and pusher and slice. For the mushrooms, wedge them in on their sides and stack them up. You must exert firm pressure or they will crumble.

To slice cheese or meat

Be sure that the cheese is cold and the meat partially frozen and cut to wedge tightly into the feed tube. Exert very firm pressure with the pusher. **Caution:** All food processors were not designed to do these chores. Those with greater horsepower can do them easily. Other machines may jam. You will have to experiment with your machine to see how these tasks are accomplished.

To "shred" cabbage and lettuce

Shop for small, tightly packed heads. Cut into wedges just large enough to force into the feed tube. For the coleslaw most people prefer, exert a very light pressure. For lettuce, use a firmer pressure because it is softer. Be certain that your pusher can be inserted at least a fraction of an inch. If it is not in place you will lose control of your slice.

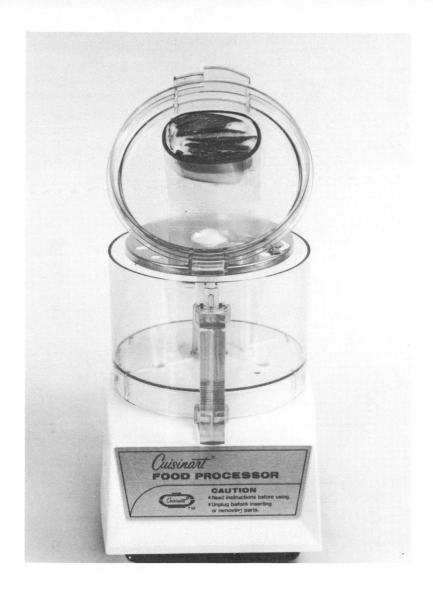

To make vegetables for dip and julienne slices

Insert a section of the wide piece of the carrot or zucchini horizontally into the feed tube. Exert firm pressure to get slices for dipping. Try to pick up the slices and replace them in order, wedging them back tightly into the bottom of the feed tube, cut side facing down. (Move the pusher out of the way several inches with your fingers). Replace the cover carefully, insert the pusher, and exert firm pressure. You will find julienne or matchstick vegetables. If you use round food like potatoes or beets you can use the cross sections to julienne.

The Shredding Disk

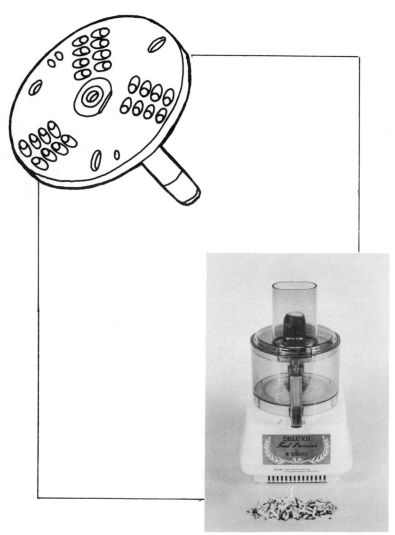

Hard or soft vegetables
If you want a short shred, stand the cleaned vegetable pieces in the feed tube and wedge tightly. If you want long firmer shreds, lay the pieces on their sides and exert firm pressure.

Soft cheeses
When shredding cheese, cut pieces to fit into the feed tube and be sure that it is cold or it will jam the machine. Exert firm pressure with the pusher. You will get long thin shreds.

26

The Plastic Blade

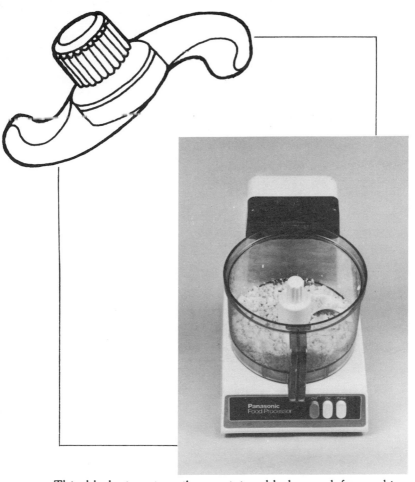

This blade is primarily a mixing blade used for making salad dressing, sauces, and combining ingredients for salads. For example, if you were making tuna salad you would chop your vegetables with the steel blade, then use the plastic blade to combine the chopped vegetables, mayonnaise and tuna. For egg salad cut the eggs in half and place them in the workbowl with the mayonnaise. Use the on/off method for both salads. The use of the plastic blade in conjunction with the on/off method helps control the pulverizing of food.

You might also like to try this blade to mix certain bread doughs. A soft egg dough will mix up very nicely with this blade. The kneading of any recipe containing more than 3 cups of flour should be finished in a larger mixing bowl.

OPTIONAL BLADES & ACCESSORIES

At the present time almost all the manufacturers of food processors produce additional blades and optional accessories, which help achieve the goals of having a food processor replace other space-hungry kitchen appliances and offering an even greater range of cutting and slicing variations. Slicing disks for thick and thin slices are avialable as are a variety of ripple cut and french fry disks. These blades enable the cook, using the same techniques described previously, to create fancy cut foods in the same simple manner.

In most cases if you own a fine slicing disk or other accessory blades you can interchange them where suggested in a recipe to give more variety. For example, try a ripple cut cucumber where a sliced one is suggested.

Accessory blades by Cuisinart.

Recently the manufacturers have outdone themselves creating the ultimate in accessories for the food processor owner. One of the most unusual and most welcome items is the potato peeling attachment for the Panasonic, which also will peel apples, onions, and grate orange rind. The vegetable sits on a disk at the top of the unit and a high dome replaces the standard lid. The vegetables are bounced around within the space and the peelings fall into the workbowl. If you are fortunate enough to have the french fry blade for this machine, french fries will frequently be on your menu.

Potato peeler by Panasonic.

Citrus lovers will be pleased to know that there is an accessory incorporating the functions of various kitchen appliances. At present there are a wealth of accessories to help us along, which will allow us to use the processor as a juicer as well. Welco has designed both a citrus juicer and vegetable juice extractor, which fit not only their unit but the two standard size Cuisinart units.

Citrus juicer by Welco.

The Whip By Waring.

One problem which always restricted the use of the food processor for whipping was limited aeration. Waring has devised an attachment which enables the cook to get full volume with egg whites and whipped cream. The whip incorporates air into the mixture with a paddle instead of cutting it out with the chopping blade.

The logistics of preparing and storing sliced and shredded food has always been a bit tricky. A battery of bowls and containers could fill the kitchen until food preparation was completed. The newest accessory on the market is the Insert-a-Bowl, a set of 2 liner bowls for the standard size machines which fit inside the regular bowl. Slice and shred into these plastic bowls, remove and set aside, or cover and refrigerate with the airtight lids, which are included. The workbowl remains clean and you can see how much and what you have processed. A must for Chinese cooking!

Insert-a-Bowl.

Once you get past the vegetable slicing stages into serious cooking and baking, a funnel is a must. There are several types available, with and without the narrow tube extension. The funnel with the tube and pusher is somewhat more useful since you can slice one carrot or banana, or even strawberries without arranging them. For cooking and baking the wide mouth of the funnel enlarges the feed tube and makes adding liquids and flour while the machine is running neater and tedious. The funnels without the tube, made by several of the machine manufacturers, give you the convenience of the latter.

Funnel with pusher.

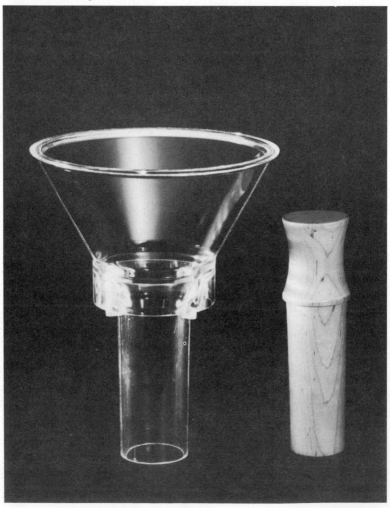

One of your most important purchases should be a storage rack for your basic and accessory blades. It is vital that you store these out of the reach of children and in a place where they are both visible and accessible. Think of them as sharp knives and store them accordingly. There are many racks available holding from 4-8 blades, with a choice of either countertop or wall models. They are available in most department stores and gourmet shops that carry the food processors.

Cuisinart 8 Blade Holder left.
Acrylic Designs Universal Blade Holder right.

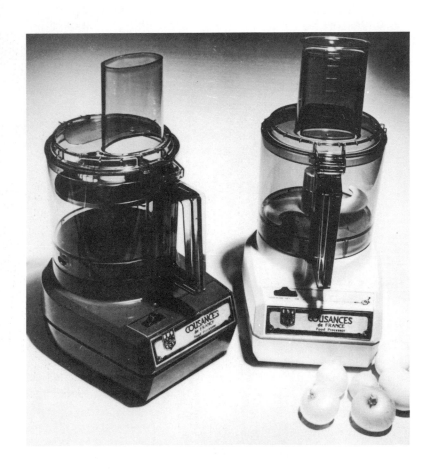

The Newest Star

At press time we became aware of a new machine which will be on the market by late spring of 1979. Presented by Cousances de France, a leader in gourmet cookware, this machine will be found predominantly in gourmet and cookware shops and will offer the serious cook the quality previously reserved for higher priced a mass market machines. If you're in the market to purchase a new machine or change to a more up to date model, check with your local cookware shop for more information.

REVISION OF RECIPES

After many years in the kitchen most cooks develop a repertoire of favorite recipes which they have prepared in the traditional manner, with hand grating of potatoes, endless and tearful mincing of onions, etc. With a small investment of time and thought food processor owners can revise and adapt their own recipes and those from standard cookbooks.

When you have a recipe with many varied ingredients, think about the ones the machine can process for you. If a recipe for stuffing calls for bread crumbs, parsley and onion, for example, the machine can do it all, without washing the bowl between processes. The trick is to start with your driest ingredients first, (bread crumbs) remove them from the bowl, then process the ones with more moisture (parsley) and end with the ones which will be the wettest or which will keep other ingredients from chopping properly. If you started with the onion, for example, the bowl would have to be wiped out before bread crumbs or parsley could be done.

Bakers are also accustomed to softening butter to room temperature before using it for baking. This is not only unnecessary when using the processor but not recommended because the soft butter will be thrown up the sides of the bowl and will have to be scraped down. Using butter straight from the refrigerator, or at room temperature for about 10 minutes will give you the best results.

In very short order you will find that you no longer have to limit yourself to a special processor cookbook. Of course the recipes in this book will make it a prominent member of your cookbook library and one to which you will refer frequently.

January: New Year's Banquet

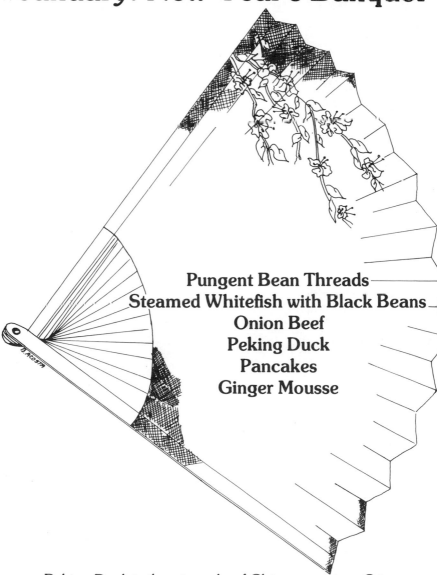

Pungent Bean Threads
Steamed Whitefish with Black Beans
Onion Beef
Peking Duck
Pancakes
Ginger Mousse

Peking Duck is the pinnacle of Chinese cuisine. Crisp duck skin and delicate meat wrapped in an oriental pancake is certainly banquet fare. The Ginger Mousse is a marvelous blend of candied ginger, cream and sherry—mmm-mmm-mmm. Your guests will be delighted with these treats from the Orient—and they are the perfect way to begin any New Year—Chinese or American!

Pungent Bean Threads

6 dried Chinese mushrooms
1/2 lbs. bean threads (fun see)
4 cups beef stock
8 water chestnuts
7 green onions
1/2 cup cold cooked ham or Chinese roast pork
2 tablespoons dark soy sauce flavoring
1/2 tablespoon sesame oil
2 eggs slightly beaten
6 tablespoons oil

Soak the mushrooms for 15 minutes in hot water, drain and remove stems. Soak the bean threads in the hot stock for 30 minutes. Drain and cut into 3" lengths using a scissor.

Insert slicing disk. Slice mushrooms, set aside. Slice the water chestnuts. Slice green onions. Slice the ham by wedging it tightly into feed tube.

Heat wok or heavy skillet to medium high heat. Add 3 tablespoons oil and stir-fry onions. Add mushrooms, water chestnuts and ham. Stir-fry for 15 seconds to combine. Add soy sauce and sesame oil. Add hot bean threads with one cup of the beef stock and mix well. Remove to a deep plate.

Scramble the eggs in 3 tablespoons of oil. Cut into thin strips. Top bean threads with scrambled eggs. Serve as a vegetable or main dish—an excellent use of leftovers.

Makes 6 to 8 servings.

Steamed White Fish with Black Beans

10 dried Chinese mushrooms
2 cloves garlic, peeled
2 slices ginger, peeled
1 1/2 tablespoons fermented black beans, washed
1 pound whitefish
4 tablespoons white wine
1/4 cup peanut oil

Sauce

1 tablespoon sesame oil
4 tablespoons light soy sauce
4 tablespoons dark soy sauce
1/2 teaspoon sugar
6 green onions, cut into 3" lengths

Soak mushrooms in hot water for 15 minutes, drain, remove stems and set aside.

Insert steel blade. With the machine running, drop garlic, ginger and black beans through the feed tube. Mince.

Have the fish cleaned and scaled, but left whole with the head and tail in place. Make 4 slits in the fish on each side where it is the thickest. Wash fish, sprinkle with wine. Place in an oiled steamer, cover and steam for 20 minutes or until cooked. Cool. Remove carefully from the steamer and place it on a serving plate.

Heat peanut oil in a small saucepan, add garlic mixture. Cook for 15 seconds. Add mushrooms, stir occasionally for 1 minute. Add sauce and green onions. Combine and cook for 15 seconds. Pour over fish, decorate with mushrooms and green onions. Cover eye with a mushroom. This is good hot or cold. (Serve with rice).

Makes 4 to 6 servings.

✓Onion Beef

1 pound flank steak,
  partially frozen
2 leeks or 1 large
  Bermuda onion
6 green onions
1 clove garlic, peeled
1 slice ginger, peeled
4 tablespoons peanut oil

Marinade
1 tablespoon cornstarch
2 tablespoons soy sauce

Sauce
1 tablespoon sesame oil
2 tablespoons sherry
2 tablespoons oyster sauce
1/2 teaspoon sugar

Insert slicing disk. Cut steak into pieces to fit the feed tube. Slice steak using heavy pressure. Set aside in a bowl and marinate for 15 minutes.

Insert slicing disk. Place leeks upright in feed tube, slice. Place green onions horizontally in feed tube, slice.

Insert steel blade. With machine running, drop garlic and ginger through feed tube, mince. Heat the wok. Add 2 tablespoons of oil. Stir-fry leeks until softened. Add green onions and stir-fry for 30 seconds. Set aside.

Heat wok. Add 2 more tablespoons peanut oil. Add ginger and garlic. Stir-fry for 30 seconds. Add flank steak, stir-fry until beef changes color. Combine sauce. Add sauce, onions and leeks. Stir for 15 seconds until beef and onions are hot and glazed. Serve with rice.

Makes 4 servings.

Peking Duck

9 green onions,
  cut into 3" lengths
1-5 pound duck
2 quarts water
4 tablespoons honey
4 slices ginger, peeled
2 stalks green onions,
  cut into 2" lengths

Garnish
pineapple chunks
Maraschino cherries

Sauce
12 tablespoons hoisin sauce
1 tablespoon sugar
1 teaspoon sesame oil

Using only the white part of the onions, cross cut at both ends. Put them in ice water to curl. Set aside. At meal time they will be used for brushes with the hoisin sauce.

Tie duck by its wings, making a loop which can be used to hang the duck. Bring water to a boil, add honey, ginger and 2 green onions. Carefully dip duck in water, scald 3 minutes on each side. Drain, pat duck dry with paper towels. Hang duck in cool airy place (perhaps a shower) for at least 4 hours. Place a pan underneath to catch any drippings.

In small saucepan, heat all sauce ingredients to boiling point. Stir. Lower heat and simmer for 30 seconds.
Preheat oven to 425°. Place an inch of water in a large shallow pan on bottom shelf of the oven. Place duck breast side up on rack in middle of oven. Roast duck for 30 minutes. Turn oven to 375°. Continue roasting the duck for about 1 hour or until it is crisp and completely cooked. Let cool at room temperature for 15 minutes. Slice skin from breast and back. Cut skin into 2" squares and arrange on heated platter. Decorate with green onion brushes. Cut off wings and drumsticks, and all the meat from duck. Arrange on another heated plate decorating with pineapple and cherries. Serve with sauce and pancakes.

Pancakes

1 3/4 cups all-purpose flour
1/4 cup cake flour
3/4 cup boiling water
1/4 cup sesame oil

Insert steel blade. Place all-purpose flour and cake flour in bowl. With machine running pour 3/4 cup boiling water and 1 teaspoon sesame oil through feed tube. Process about 8 seconds until a dough ball forms. Let rest in covered greased bowl for 20 minutes. Roll into sausage shape and cut into 18 pieces. Knead each piece adding more flour as needed. Roll each piece between your fingers to make a smooth ball. Flatten one ball, cover lightly one side with sesame oil and join with second ball. Flatten with hand. Using a rolling pin, roll out the flattened balls into a circle keeping as uniform as possible. It should be about 5" in diameter. Place a skillet on the stove and brush with sesame oil. Add one of the double pancakes. Cook briefly (about 30 seconds.) Turn it over and repeat on second side. Try not to overcook. Carefully pull the pancakes apart into 2 single pancakes. Repeat process until all pancakes are made. They may be frozen or kept in aluminum foil until serving time. To reheat you may steam them in a steamer or heat in a 325° oven about 10 minutes.

To serve: Have pancakes, sauce and onion brushes ready. Place a pancake on your plate. Brush sauce on pancake with onion brush. Place a piece of duck skin and duck meat on top of brush. Roll pancake and eat it with your fingers. You are enjoying one of the great delicacies of the Oriental world.

Makes 4 servings.

Ginger Mousse

1/2 cup candied ginger
2 slices fresh ginger, peeled
3 cups milk
2 envelopes unflavored gelatin
3/4 cup sugar
1 teaspoon freshly grated nutmeg
4 teaspoons cornstarch
2 tablespoons sherry
3 eggs separated
2/3 cup heavy cream
3 kumquats, cut in slivers

Insert steel blade. With machine running, drop candied ginger and fresh ginger through the feed tube. Chop. Set aside.

Combine milk, gelatin and 1/2 cup of the sugar in a medium saucepan. Stir while heating to a simmer. Continue stirring until gelatin dissolves. Stir in nutmeg and ginger.

Blend cornstarch and sherry. Add to mixture. Continue cooking. Stir constantly until mixture thickens. Beat in yolks stirring constantly. Remove from heat, cool. With mixer beat egg whites until stiff. Fold into yolk mixture. Whip cream until stiff, add remaining sugar. Fold into mousse mixture.

Lightly oil inside of an eight cup mold. Pour mousse into mold. Refrigerate several hours before serving. Top with slivered kumquats and extra whipped cream.

Makes 10 to 12 servings.

February: Pacific Spectacle for "The Boss"

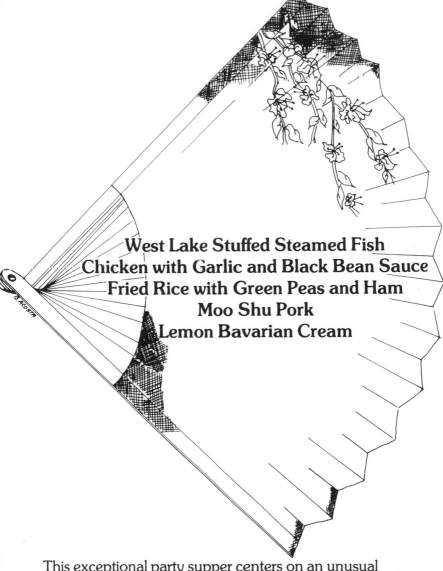

West Lake Stuffed Steamed Fish
Chicken with Garlic and Black Bean Sauce
Fried Rice with Green Peas and Ham
Moo Shu Pork
Lemon Bavarian Cream

This exceptional party supper centers on an unusual stuffed fish accompanied by a complimentary side dish of Moo Shu Pork. In Chinese banquet style the meal also calls for Garlic Chicken and Fried Rice. The lemon dessert refreshes the palate and helps with digestion.

West Lake Stuffed Steamed Fish

1 lb. whitefish, cleaned,
head and tail left intact*
3 tablespoons peanut oil
4 green onions, sliced

Marinade
2 tablespoons light soy sauce
1 tablespoon wine

Stuffing
2 ribs celery, cut in to thirds
1 slice fresh ginger, peeled
1/4 cup water chestnuts
1/2 cup bamboo shoots
4 dried mushrooms
1 cup cooked ham

Seasoning
1 teaspoon white wine
1 teaspoon light soy sauce
1/4 teaspoon salt
1/8 teaspoon pepper
1/4 teaspoon sugar
1 teaspoon cornstarch

Sauce
1/2 teaspoon light soy sauce
2/3 cup chicken broth
1 teaspoon sesame oil
1 tablespoon cornstarch
mixed with
3 tablespoons water
4 shredded green onions;
sliced.

Insert slicing blade. Wedge celery into feed tube and slice with medium pressure. Set aside.

Insert steel blade. With machine running, drop ginger through feed tube and mince. Leaving ginger in bowl, add water chestnuts, and bamboo shoots. Chop. Set aside. Soak mushrooms in hot water for 15 minutes. Rinse, squeeze out water, remove stems and place in processor and chop. Add to bamboo shoots. Place ham in bowl, chop. Mix with bamboo shoots. Combine all stuffing ingredients. Combine all seasoning ingredients and mix together with stuffing.

Heat wok or heavy skillet, add peanut oil. Add stuffing and stir-fry 2 minutes, remove from heat. Mix marinade ingredients together and rub on fish. Stuff fish. Place fish on its side in a lightly oiled steamer, making sure the water in the steamer stays below the fish. Cover and steam at high heat for 10 to 15 minutes or until fish is cooked. Heat sauce ingredients and stir until thickened. Remove fish carefully from steamer to serving platter, pour sauce over fish. Garnish with green onion.

*Have fishmonger enlarge opening on underside of cavity. Makes 4 to 6 servings.

Chicken with Garlic and Black Bean Sauce

2 tablespoons fermented black beans, rinsed
1 slice ginger, peeled
3 cloves garlic
2 1/2 pound chicken, cut into bite sized pieces
     (or 2 whole chicken breasts)
1/2 teaspoon salt
3 tablespoons peanut oil
3 stalks green onions, cut into 3" lengths

Sauce

1/2 teaspoon salt
2 tablespoons dark soy sauce
1 teaspoon cornstarch

Insert steel blade. With the machine running, drop the black beans, ginger, garlic and salt through the feed tube, mince.

Heat 3 tablespoons of oil in the wok or heavy skillet. Add bean mixture and stir-fry for 30 seconds. Add chicken. Combine sauce ingredients and add. Cover wok. Simmer over low heat until the gravy has thickened and chicken has cooked about 5 minutes.

Insert slicing blade. Place green onions in the feed tube horizontally, slice. Sprinkle green onions over chicken and simmer 30 seconds. Serve hot with rice.

Makes 4 servings.

Fried Rice with Green Peas and Ham

1 clove garlic, peeled
1 cup ham, cut into 1/2"
  pieces
1 large onion, pared, cut
  into quarters
2 tablespoons cold water
6 cups cold cooked rice
1 cup cooked peas
3 extra large eggs, slightly
  beaten
3 tablespoons peanut oil

Sauce
3 tablespoons light soy sauce
1 tablespoon wine
1/4 teaspoon salt
1/8 teaspoon pepper
1 tablespoon cornstarch

Insert steel blade. With machine running drop garlic through the feed tube, mince. Add ham, and chop using ON/OFF motion. Set aside.

Insert slicing blade. Slice the onion.

Add 2 tablespoons cold water to the cold cooked rice. Loosen and separate the grains. Heat large skillet, add oil and onions and stir-fry until they are soft. Add ham and garlic. Stir-fry 30 seconds. Add rice, cook for 2 minutes stirring constantly. Add eggs. Stir until they are absorbed. Combine sauce ingredients. Stir in. Add peas. Cook 1 minute more tossing all ingredients thoroughly. Serve hot.

Makes 12 servings.

Fried rice is an excellent way to use leftovers. Various kinds of cooked meat and vegetables may be cut into fine shreds and added to this dish.

Moo Shu Pork

10 oz. pork loin-partially
    frozen, cut into pieces
    that will fit into feed tube
4 green onions, cut into
    3" lengths
1 slice ginger, peeled
1/3 cup golden needles
    (dried lily buds)
1/4 cup wood ears
1/2 cup bamboo shoots
4 extra large eggs
1/4 teaspoon salt
5 tablespoons peanut oil
Pancakes (See recipe for Peking Duck)

Sauce
3 tablespoons light soy sauce
1 tablespoon dark soy sauce
2 tablespoons wine
2 tablespoons chicken stock
1 teaspoon sesame oil
1/2 teaspoon salt
1/4 teaspoon pepper
1 teaspoon cornstarch

2/3 cup hoisin sauce
green onions, slivered

Soak golden needles and wood ears in hot water for 15 minutes, drain.

Insert slicing blade. Slice the golden needles and wood ears together, with medium pressure. Set aside. Slice bamboo shoots (if not presliced) using light pressure. Set aside.

Reinsert slicing blade. Wedge pork into feed tube and slice using firm pressure. Set aside.

Reinsert slicing blade. Place green onions in the feed tube horizontally, slice. Set aside.

Heat 2 tablespoons of peanut oil in wok over moderate heat. Add the beaten eggs and salt and scramble lightly. Remove and set aside.

Add remaining 3 tablespoons peanut oil to the wok. When oil is hot, add ginger and remove when brown. Add green onions. Stir-fry for 30 seconds. Add pork and stir-fry until pork is cooked. Add golden needles and wood ears and stir-fry 30 seconds. Add bamboo shoots and mix well. Add sauce and scrambled eggs. Toss and mix well. Transfer to heated platter.

Serve with pancakes or rice, hoisin sauce and slivered onions. Each person takes a pancake, adds some Moo Shu Pork and slivered green onions. Spread 1 tablespoon hoisin on top of pancake and roll. Eat and enjoy a great treat!

Makes 4 to 6 servings.

Golden Lemon Cream

1 large lemon
1/2 cup sugar
1 envelope unflavored gelatin
3/4 cup cold water
2 jumbo eggs separated
1/4 teaspoon salt
1 can frozen lemonade, thawed
1 cup heavy cream, whipped *
Strawberries for garnish, optional

Remove peel from lemon, being careful not to include the white part.

Insert steel blade. Add peel and 1/4 cup sugar to bowl, mince. Add gelatin, water, egg yolks, and salt. Combine with 1 ON/OFF turn. Place mixture in saucepan over low heat. Stir constantly until mixture is slightly thickened, about 4 minutes.

Remove pan from the stove, add the lemonade and stir. Chill, stirring occasionally, until mixture mounds slightly when dropped from spoon. With electric mixer beat egg whites until frothy. Gradually add remaining 1/4 cup sugar and continue beating whites until stiff. Fold into gelatin mixture. Fold in whipped cream. Turn into lightly greased 5 cup mold. Chill until firm. Garnish with strawberries.

Makes 6 to 8 servings.

*If you wish to whip the cream in the processor be sure that the bowl, steel blade, and cream are chilled thoroughly. The cream will take about 2 minutes to whip and will be very heavy and thick, unlike cream whipped by hand or with an electric mixer.

March: New Neighbors "Welcome" Dinner

Deep Fried Shrimp Toast
Hot and Sour Soup
Beef with Oyster Sauce and Vegetables
Minced Pigeon with Chinese Pancakes
Green Pea Cake

A menu from northern China, this is the ultimate in elegant taste. The advantage of this meal is that most of it can be made ahead—the shrimp toast freezes well, the soup can be made the day before as can the green pea cake (a most unusual taste sensation). The hostess can really enjoy herself yet the guest dine on a very adventuresome foods.

Deep Fried Shrimp Toast

1 slice ginger, peeled
1/2 pound raw shrimp, shelled, washed and deveined
2 oz. pork fat
1 egg white
1/8 teaspoon salt
1/2 tablespoon wine
1 tablespoon cornstarch
6 slices white bread, crusts removed
3 cups peanut oil
4 tablespoons black sesame seeds for decoration,
    optional

Insert steel blade. With machine running, drop ginger through feed tube, mince.

Add shrimp to processor bowl. Add fat, egg white, salt, wine and cornstarch to processor bowl. Mince using ON/OFF method.

Cut each slice of bread into 4 pieces. Place 1/2 tablespoon shrimp mixture on each piece of bread and spread evenly to the edges. Heat oil to 380° in wok or heavy skillet. Fry shrimp toast face side down, 10 seconds, turn over and fry for 5 seconds. Fry only 4 at a time. Remove with slotted spoon, drain on paper toweling. Serve hot. Decorate with black sesame seeds. Arrange the toast on lettuce leaves and decorate attractively with parsley. These freeze well.

Makes 24 shrimp toast.

Hot and Sour Soup

4 cups chicken broth
1 green onion, cut into
   1 1/2" pieces
4 Chinese dried mushrooms
1 tablespoon tree ears
1 tablespoon tiger lily buds
1/2 cup bamboo shoots
1/3 cup lean pork or
   chicken, cooked
   and partially frozen
1/2 cup bean curd, cut
   into 1/2" pieces
2 extra large eggs,
   slightly beaten

Seasoning

3 tablespoons wine vinegar
1/2 teaspoon pepper
1 tablespoon sesame oil

Flavoring

1 tablespoon light soy sauce
1/2 teaspoon sugar
3/4 teaspoon salt

3 tablespoons cornstarch
   combined with
3 tablespoons cold water

In large serving bowl combine vinegar, pepper and sesame oil. Set aside until ready to serve.

Insert slicing disk. Slice green onion. Set aside. Soak mushrooms, tree ears and tiger lily buds in hot water for 20 minutes. Pinch off tough parts of mushrooms.

Insert slicing disk. Slice mushrooms, tree ears and tiger lily buds. Slice bamboo shoots. Set aside.

Insert slicing disk. Slice pork using firm pressure.

Bring broth to a simmer in large saucepan. Add pork, mushrooms, bean curd, bamboo shoots, tree ears and tiger lily buds and simmer for 3 minutes. Add flavoring. Add cornstarch mixture and green onion. Bring soup to boil. Pour eggs in slowly and turn off heat. Pour into prepared serving bowl which contains vinegar, pepper and sesame oil. Serve hot.

Makes 8 to 10 servings.

Beef with Oyster Sauce and Vegetables

1 pound flank steak,
  partially frozen
1 clove garlic, peeled
1 slice ginger, peeled
6 green onions, cut in 2" pieces

Marinade
2 tablespoons dark soy sauce
1 tablespoon cornstarch
1/4 teaspoon sugar

1 large tomato
1 green pepper, halved
4 tablespoons peanut oil

Sauce
5 tablespoons oyster sauce
1/2 tablespoon sugar
2 tablespoons wine
1 tablespoon cornstarch

Insert slicing disk. Cut meat into pieces to wedge into feed tube. Slice using firm pressure. Combine marinade ingredients in bowl and add meat. Marinate for 20 minutes.

Insert steel blade. With the machine running, drop garlic, ginger and green onions through the feed tube and mince.

Insert slicing disk. Slice pepper.

Slice tomato into 8 sections by hand. Heat oil in wok or in heavy skillet. Add garlic mixture and stir-fry for 30 seconds. Add meat and stir-fry until it changes color. Add tomatoes and pepper. Combine with sauce ingredients. Serve hot with rice or noodles.

Makes 4 servings.

Minced Pigeon with Chinese Pancakes

1 pigeon or 1/2 pound chicken thighs
or rock cornish hen
6 oz. pork, cut into 1/2" cubes
2 chicken livers
1 clove garlic, peeled
1/2 teaspoon dried
chopped hot peppers
3 tablespoons cooked
peas
5 dried mushrooms
1 large onion, cut
into quarters
1 cup water chestnuts
4 oz. bean threads
3 cups peanut oil

Marinade
1 tablespoon light soy
sauce
1/2 teaspoon salt
1 egg yolk
2 teaspoons cornstarch
1/2 teaspoon sugar

Sauce
1 tablespoon soy sauce
1 tablespoon chicken stock
1 teaspoon cornstarch
1 teaspoon salt
1 teaspoon sesame oil
1/4 teaspoon black pepper

24 Chinese pancakes (see
Peking Duck recipe page 42)
or lettuce leaves may be
substituted

Remove bones from poultry and cut into chunks.
Place in bowl.

Insert steel blade. Place poultry, pork and liver
in bowl. Use ON/OFF turns and mince until very fine.
Marinate 15 minutes.

Soak dried mushrooms in warm water for 15 minutes.
Discard stems.

Insert Steel blade. Chop mushrooms. Set aside.
Chop onion and water chestnuts together.

Heat oil to 380° in wok. Fry bean threads on each side for only 3 seconds. Remove to serving platter and let cool, then crush with hand.

Insert steel blade. With machine running drop garlic and hot pepper through feed tube and mince.

Remove all but 3 tablespoons of oil in wok and heat. Add garlic and pepper. Stir-fry for 15 seconds. Add onion and water chestnuts. Stir-fry until onions are soft about 2 minutes. Add mushrooms and stir-fry 30 seconds. Add meat mixture. Combine sauce ingredients and add. Stir-fry until cooked. Add green peas. Pour over fried bean threads. Serve with Chinese pancakes or with lettuce leaves, cut into 2 1/2" round pieces. Wrap pancakes around meat and bean thread mixture.

Makes 6 servings.

Green Pea Cake

1 package unflavored gelatin
1/4 cup cold water
1 large can green peas (17 oz.)
1 cup sugar
1 cup heavy cream, whipped
1/2 teaspoon vanilla
1/2 cup heavy cream, whipped
1/3 cup candied cherries

Soften gelatin in water. Drain green peas.

Insert steel blade. Add green peas, and puree.

In medium saucepan add sugar to gelatin mixture. Bring to a boil and reduce heat. Add green peas and mix well. Simmer for 3 minutes. Cool. When mixture begins to thicken, fold in 1 cup whipped cream. Mix with vanilla. Pour into mold or tall glasses. Refrigerate until set.

When ready to serve, top with whipped cream and garnish with cherries.

Makes 6 to 8 servings.

April: "Eight Precious Friends" Dinner

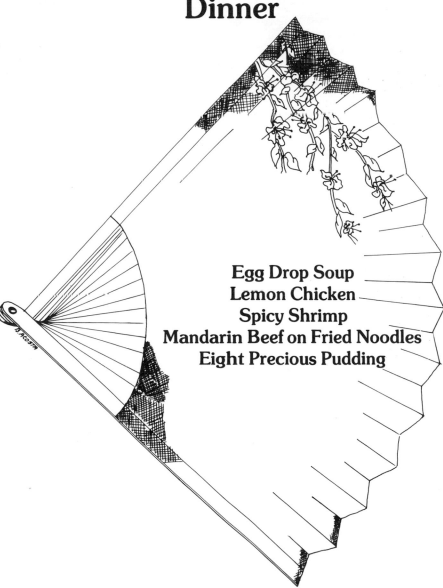

Egg Drop Soup
Lemon Chicken
Spicy Shrimp
Mandarin Beef on Fried Noodles
Eight Precious Pudding

This light meal is perfect for springtime entertaining. With no heavy sauces, the tastes are classic. Eight Precious Pudding is often served on special occasions—it contains eight different fruits which are laced with a tangy lemon sauce.

Egg Drop Soup

3 extra large eggs
3 green onions
1 quart chicken broth
1/4 teaspoon salt
1/8 teaspoon pepper
2 tablespoons cornstarch
1 teaspoon sugar

Insert plastic blade. Mix eggs. Set aside.

Insert slicing disk. If you have a funnel with tube and pusher, cut the green onion in 1/2 and slice in the funnel. If you don't have the funnel, slice them by hand.

Mix cornstarch with 4 tablespoons of the chicken broth. Using large saucepan, heat remaining chicken broth to a simmer. Stir in salt, pepper, cornstarch and sugar. Bring soup to rapid boil, add green onion. Drop the beaten eggs from a tablespoon in a slow stream. Shut off heat. The eggs will form shreds in the hot broth. Serve in individual bowls.

Makes 6 to 8 servings.

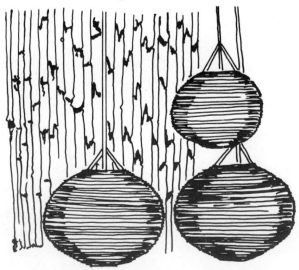

Lemon Chicken

2 whole chicken breasts,
   split, boned, with skin on
1/4 teaspoon salt
1/8 teaspoon pepper
1 tablespoon sherry
juice of 1/2 lemon
3 cups peanut oil

Sauce
3 tablespons catsup
2 tablespoons light soy
   sauce
1 tablespoon sesame oil
3 tablespoons vinegar
3 tablespoons sugar

Batter
4 tablespons cornstarch
4 tablespoons flour
1/2 teaspoon baking
   powder

Garnish
1/2 head iceberg lettuce
   cut into wedges
1 lemon, unpeeled
1 cup cherry tomatoes
1/2 cup parsley

Sprinkle salt, pepper, sherry and juice of 1/2 lemon over chicken breast and marinate for 20 minutes.

Mix batter. Drain chicken and coat with batter. Heat peanut oil to 380°. Fry chicken until golden brown. Drain on paper toweling, cut into bite size pieces.

Insert plastic blade. Add sauce ingredients, mix well. Heat 2 tablespoons oil in small saucepan, add sauce, cook and stir until hot.

Insert slicing disk. With light pressure, slice lettuce. Set aside. Cut top and bottom off lemon. Slice lemon, set aside. Arrange lettuce on a serving plate. Arrange chicken on lettuce. Pour hot sauce over chicken and decorate with lemon, tomatoes and parsley.

Makes 4 servings.

A great meal for children. They seem to enjoy the lemony taste very much.

Spicy Shrimp

3 cups raw shrimp
2 teaspoons salt
1 slice ginger, peeled
1 clove garlic, peeled
3 green onions, cut into
  2" lengths
2 cups peanut oil

Marinade

1 tablespoon sherry
1 egg white
1 tablespoon cornstarch

Sauce

2 tablespoons hot
  bean sauce
5 tablespoons ketchup
1 tablespoon light soy
  sauce
1 tablespoon sugar
1 1/2 teaspoons vinegar
1/2 teaspoon salt
1/2 cup chicken stock
2 tablespoons cornstarch

Wash, shell and remove black veins from the shrimp. Sprinkle the shrimp with salt, wash and drain. Combine marinade ingredients. Mix with shrimp and set aside.

Insert steel blade. With machine running, drop the ginger, garlic and green onion through the feed tube, mince. Set aside.

Insert plastic blade. Add sauce ingredients, blend. Heat the oil to 380°, add shrimp. As soon as they change color, remove from oil and drain on paper toweling. Remove all but 2 tablespoons oil from wok.

Heat remaining oil in wok or heavy skillet. Add ginger mixture, stir-fry for 30 seconds. Add sauce and shrimp, stirring constantly until thickened. Remove to serving plate. Serve with white rice.

Makes 4 servings.

Mandarin Beef on Fried Noodles

1 pound flank steak,
  partially frozen
1/2 green pepper
1/2 cup bamboo shoots
2 green onion, cut
  into 2" lengths
1 clove garlic, peeled
1 slice ginger, peeled
4 oz. bean threads
2 cups peanut oil

Marinade
1/4 teaspoon salt
1/2 egg white
2 teaspoons cornstarch

Sauce
1/2 teaspoon sugar
2 teaspoons white wine
1 tablespoon chili paste
  with garlic
1 teaspoon sesame oil

Insert slicing disk. Using heavy pressure, slice meat. Place in a medium bowl with marinade for 15 minutes.

Insert slicing disk. Slice green pepper, bamboo shoots and green onions, with medium pressure. Set aside.

Insert steel blade. With machine running, drop the garlic and ginger through the feed tube, mince. Set aside.

Insert plastic blade. Add sauce ingredients, combine 2 seconds.

Add beef to 2 cups of hot oil Blanch until beef loses its red color. Remove to a bowl.

Loosen the bean threads by pulling apart. Heat the oil to 380°, fry them on both sides until puffy, about 2 seconds on each side. Drain on paper toweling. Place on serving platter in a bird nest shape.

Remove all but 3 tablespoons of the oil and reheat. Add garlic and ginger, stir-fry 15 seconds. Then add pepper, bamboo shoots and onion and stir-fry several minutes.

Add sauce to wok. Stir to combine. Transfer to the fried noodles, serve hot.

Makes 4 servings.

Eight Precious Pudding

2 tablespoons butter
2 cups dried fruit (as dates, plums, candied oranges
  and lemon peel, cherries, raisins, currants or nuts)
2 cups cooked rice
8 tablespoons sugar
4 tablespoons butter, softened
3 tablespoons raisins

Use 6 cup bowl or mold and coat with 2 tablespoons butter. Arrange dried fruits and nuts in the bowl in a decorative fashion covering the sides and bottom of the bowl. Start at the bottom of bowl and work up to the top.

Mix rice with sugar, butter and raisins. Carefully spoon rice mixture into the bowl, press lightly but firmly to hold in place. Cover top with foil. Press in steamer and steam for 20 minutes. Unmold on serving platter. Serve warm with lemon sauce. This rice mold freezes well.

Lemon Sauce

rind of 1 lemon
1/2 cup sugar
2 1/4 cups water
2 tablespoons butter
2 tablespoons cornstarch
2 tablespoons lemon juice
2 drops yellow food coloring, optional

Insert steel blade. Add rind and sugar, chop. Combine 2 cups of the water, sugar, and butter in a medium saucepan. Bring to a boil, reduce heat to simmer. Blend cornstarch with 1/4 cup water, add to sauce. Stir until it thickens. Add lemon juice and coloring. Serve with the hot unmolded pudding. Guests help themselves to the lemon sauce.

The tart lemon taste helps to balance the sweetness of the pudding and the two tastes blend to make a remarkable taste treat. This is a spectacular dessert.

Makes 8 to 10 servings.

May: May Pole Feast

Velvety Chicken Corn Soup
Striped Bass with Orange and Cucumbers
Broccoli with Brown Sugar
Stir-Fried Asparagus with Beef
Sweet Potato Balls
Drunken Pears

Color plays an important role in this hot weather meal. The variety of foods and colors is breathtaking. You can continue the panoply with bright paper plates, napkins, fresh flowers and chopsticks—of course!

Velvety Chicken Corn Soup

1 whole chicken breast, cooked, cut into 1" cubes
2 tablespoons minced ham or crab
1 tablespoon cornstarch
3 cups chicken broth
1 teaspoon salt
1-8 oz. can creamed corn
1 tablespoon dry sherry
2 egg whites

Insert steel blade. Mince chicken using ON/OFF motion. Remove chicken, set aside. Put ham in bowl and mince using ON/OFF motion.

Dissolve cornstarch in 2 tablespoons cold water. Place chicken broth in medium-sized saucepan and bring to a simmer. Add salt, creamed corn and sherry. Simmer for 3 minutes. Add dissolved cornstarch and stir for 1 minute. Quickly stir in the chicken, then sprinkle in the ham.

Beat egg white until slightly foamy. Add to soup. Heat until egg is cooked. Place in individual bowls and serve hot.

Makes 6 servings.

Striped Bass with Orange and Cucumbers

1 whole striped bass or trout
6 slices ginger root, peeled
rinds of 2 oranges
6 sweet white cucumbers
6 sprigs Chinese parsley
3 green onions

Sauce

1/4 cup light soy sauce
1/4 cup dry white wine
1/2 teaspoon dark soy sauce
1/2 teaspoon sesame oil
1/4 cup peanut oil

Place cleaned and scaled whole striped bass on serving plate.

Insert steel blade. With machine running, drop ginger and orange rind through feed tube and mince. Place fish on dish, sprinkle ginger and orange over fish. Place fish plate in a steamer and steam for 15 minutes or until cooked. Check doneness by inserting chopstick next to backbone. Drain off juice.

Insert steel blade. Chop parsley using ON/OFF motion. Chop green onions. Set aside.

Insert slicing disk. Slice cucumbers lengthwise. Sprinkle parsley, onion and cucumber on top of fish. Combine sauce ingredients and heat in small saucepan. Pour over fish. Serve hot with rice or noodles.

Makes 4 servings.

Broccoli with Brown Sugar ✓

1 slice ginger, peeled
1 clove garlic, peeled
3 tablespoons oil
1 lb. broccoli cut into
1/2" by 2" pieces,
blanched

1 teaspoon cornstarch
combined with
2 tablespoons water

Sauce

2 tablespoons thin soy sauce
1 tablespoon dark soy sauce
2 tablespoons brown sugar
1 teaspoon sesame seed oil

Insert steel blade. With machine running, drop the ginger and garlic through the feed tube and mince about 3 seconds. Set aside.

Insert plastic blade. Combine sauce ingredients for about 4 seconds.

Heat wok or heavy skillet and add 3 tablespoons oil. When oil is hot, brown garlic and ginger. Add blanched broccoli and lower heat. Add sauce and cornstarch, stirring until the sauce thickens slightly. Serve hot.

Makes 4 servings.

Stir-Fried Asparagus with Beef

1 pound flank steak,
   partially frozen
rind of 1 orange
1/2 cup walnut
   halves, broken
1 clove garlic, peeled
2 slice ginger, peeled
1/2 pound fresh asparagus,
   cut into 2" pieces
1 tablespoon cornstarch
3 tablespoons peanut oil
1 1/2 tablespoons sesame oil

Marinade
4 tablespoons dark soy sauce
1/3 cup sherry

Insert slicing disk. Cut steak into pieces that will wedge into feed tube. Slice flank steak, using firm pressure. Marinate meat in soy sauce and sherry for 15 minutes in mixing bowl. Wash and dry bowl.

Insert steel blade. Add orange rind and walnuts, chop coarsely. Set aside.

Insert steel blade. With the machine running drop garlic and ginger through the feed tube. Mince about 5 seconds.

Parboil asparagus for 2 minutes, drain. Remove the meat from marinade. Add cornstarch to marinade.

Heat wok, or heavy skillet. Add oil, stir-fry beef until it changes color. Remove to a plate. Add minced garlic and ginger to wok and stir to combine. Add asparagus and mix. Add beef and stir-fry. Add marinade and orange mixture. Stir-fry until glazed and bubbling. Add sesame oil to wok and serve.

Makes 4 servings.

Sweet Potato Balls

1 1/2 pounds sweet potatoes *
5 tablespoons sugar
1/2 cup flour
1/4 teaspoon salt
1 egg
2 cups peanut oil
1/4 cup powdered sugar

Wash and peel sweet potatoes, steam or boil over high heat until very soft.

Insert plastic blade. Whip potatoes using ON/OFF motion. Add sugar, flour, salt and egg, mix 5 seconds. Form small balls by using a tablespoon.

Heat oil in 380°. Deep fry the potato balls (6 at a time) over medium heat until slightly brown. Using a slotted spoon, drain on paper toweling, sprinkle with powdered sugar. Keep warm on a serving plate in a 325° oven until you are ready to serve.

Makes 6 servings.

*It is also possible to use canned sweet potatoes. In that case, drain and put into processor using steel blade. Continue as described above.

Drunken Pears

1/2 cup dates, chilled
1/2 cup walnuts
6 large pears, peeled and cored
1/3 cup brown sugar
1 cup sauterne

Insert steel blade. Chop dates and walnuts using ON/OFF motion.

Fill cavity of pears with the mixture of chopped dates and walnuts. Put pears in a greased casserole. Sprinkle with 1/3 cup brown sugar and pour 1 cup sauterne over pears. Cover casserole and bake in a 325° oven for 45 minutes or until pears are tender.

Makes 6 servings.

May: Mother's Day Dinner— Cooked Without Mother

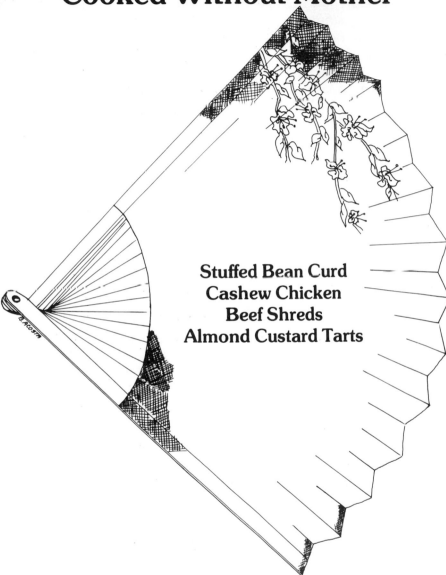

Stuffed Bean Curd
Cashew Chicken
Beef Shreds
Almond Custard Tarts

This is a relatively easy menu which would be perfect for father and/or children to prepare. The ingredients are authentic, yet the processes are simple enough even for young children. And of course Mother could have no finer gift than a dinner prepared by the family.

Stuffed Bean Curd

3/4 lb. lean pork, chilled and cut into 1" cubes
8 water chestnuts
1 green onion cut into 1 1/2" lengths
1 large egg
2 tablespoons light soy sauce
1/2 teaspoon salt
2 cups oil

Insert steel blade. Add pork to bowl. Mince using ON/OFF technique. Set aside. Add water chestnuts, green onion, egg, soy sauce, and salt to work bowl and mince. Combine with pork. Slit one corner of bean curd and stuff with pork mixture.

Heat oil to 380° in heavy skillet or wok. Fry bean curd until meat is cooked. Drain on paper toweling. Serve hot.

Cashew Chicken

2 chicken breasts, boned,
   skinned and partially frozen
1/4 cup oil
2 cloves ginger, peeled
1 clove garlic, peeled
1 cup cashews
1/2 cup bamboo shoots,
   drained

Marinade
2 tablespoons white wine
1/4 cup light soy sauce

Thickening
2 tablespoons cornstarch
1 cup water

Insert slicing blade. Slice chicken breasts. Place in marinade for 20 minutes.

Using large heavy skillet heat oil. Saute cashews for 1 minute. Drain on paper toweling.

Insert steel blade. With the machine running, drop ginger and garlic through the feed tube, mince. Remove.

Insert steel blade. Place cashews in work bowl. Using 3 ON/OFF turns, coarsely chop the cashews.

Remove all but 3 tablespoons of oil from skillet. Heat oil. Stir-fry ginger and garlic for 30 seconds. Add chicken and stir-fry until browned. Add thickening mixture, cover and simmer for 15 minutes.

Insert slicing blade. Slice bamboo shoots.

Add bamboo shoots and cashews. Stir-fry until combined. Serve hot with rice.

Makes 4 servings.

Beef Shreds

1 lb. flank steak
   partially frozen
2 slices ginger, peeled
1 clove garlic, peeled
1 large carrot, peeled
6 stalks celery, cut in thirds
1/2 teaspoon salt
1 tablespoon red pepper flakes

Marinade
3 tablespoons dark soy sauce
1 teaspoon white wine

Insert slicing blade. * Wedge pieces of steak in feed tube and slice, using firm pressure. Stack up pieces and cut lengthwise using cleaver or chef's knife. Marinate for 15 minutes. Heat oil to 380° in wok or heavy skillet. Stir-fry meat until it is almost cooked. Drain on paper toweling.

Insert steel blade. With the machine running drop the ginger and garlic through the feed tube and process until minced. Set aside.

Insert shredding blade. Shred carrot. Set aside.

Insert slicing blade. Wedge pieces of celery into feed tube tightly and slice. Set aside.

Remove all but 3 tablespoons of the oil from the wok. Stir-fry ginger and garlic for 30 seconds. Add red pepper and salt. Stir to combine. Add carrot and celery and stir-fry until meat is cooked or about 1 minute. Serve hot with rice.

Makes 4 servings.

*If you have a thin slicing blade you could use it to slice the meat and celery.

Almond Custard Tarts

2 cups all-purpose flour
1/2 teaspoon sugar
1/2 teaspoon salt
8 tablespoons cold lard, cut into chunks
6 or 7 tablespoons ice water
1 1/4 cups milk, scalded
1 cup sugar
3/4 teaspoon almond extract
4 extra large egg yolks, slightly beaten

Preheat oven to 400°.

Insert steel blade. Add flour, sugar, salt, and lard to bowl. With the machine running pour ice water through feed tube and process until a dough ball begins to form. Gather all dough together into a ball. Cover with plastic wrap and chill for 1 hour.

Roll out dough on lightly floured board to 1/4" thickness. Cut with 4" round cutter. Press circles into 2" muffin pans. Chill while preparing the filling.

Using a medium saucepan add milk, sugar and almond extract. Cook over low heat until sugar dissolves. Cool. Using a wisk beat 1/3 cup of the cooled mixture into egg yolks. Pour eggs yolks into milk mixture in a very slow stream until the two are combined. Stir until smooth. Pour custard into pastry lined pans and fill 3/4 full. Bake in preheated oven about 20 minutes or until top is golden brown. Remove to a wire rack to cool. Serve cooled.

Makes about 16 tarts.

June: Mandarin Picnic

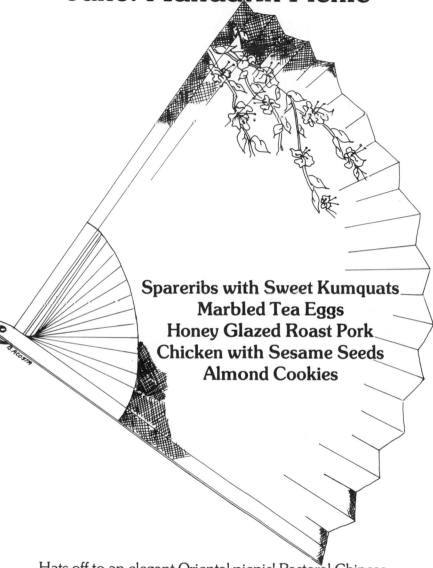

Spareribs with Sweet Kumquats
Marbled Tea Eggs
Honey Glazed Roast Pork
Chicken with Sesame Seeds
Almond Cookies

Hats off to an elegant Oriental picnic! Pastoral Chinese
dining is done in high style—where the utensils must be
worthy of the food. Ivory chopsticks, porcelain cups and
china plates are packed for the outing. A red tablecloth
carries through the oriental theme and signifies a most
festive occasion. For added flair tuck a paper parasol
into each folded napkin. All food can be made ahead
and transported to your favorite lotus garden.

Spareribs with Sweet Kumquats

2 pounds spareribs, separated
3 slices ginger root, peeled
5 green onions, cut in 2" lengths
1/2 cup cornstarch
3 cups peanut oil
1 1/2 cups sweet kumquats, drained

Marinade
2 tablespoons wine
2 tablespoons light soy sauce

Sauce
1 tablespoon wine
2 tablespoons sugar
2 1/2 tablespoons vinegar
1/2 teaspoon salt
1 teaspoon cornstarch
2 tablespoons water

Insert steel blade. With machine running drop ginger and onions through feed tube, chop. Set aside.

Sprinkle marinade over ribs. Marinate for 20 minutes.

Insert plastic blade. Add sauce ingredients and combine.

Coat spareribs with cornstarch. Heat oil to 380°. Fry spareribs for 10 minutes or until golden brown. When cool remove all but 1 tablespoon oil from the wok. Heat wok, saute green onions and ginger for 15 seconds. Add sauce and stir until it thickens. Add fried spareribs and kumquats. Serve hot.

Makes 4 servings.

Marbled Tea Eggs

8 jumbo eggs
3 dark tea bags
3 tablespoons dark soy sauce
3 teaspoons salt
1 star anise or 1/2 teaspoon cinnamon
2 1/2 cups cold water
1/2 head of lettuce, cut into wedges

In saucepan cover eggs with cold water and cook over medium heat for 20 minutes. Chill cooked eggs in cold water until cooled. Crack the egg shells with the back of a tablespoon without removing the shells.

In a saucepan combine cold water with all remaining ingredients, except lettuce. Add the eggs and cook for 30 minutes over low heat. Set aside until the eggs are cold. Then remove egg shells carefully before serving.

Insert slicing disk. Slice lettuce. Make a nest of lettuce on a plate. Place eggs in the nest and serve with salt.

Makes 8 servings.

Honey Glazed Roast Pork

2 lb. lean pork roast
6 tablespoons honey
2 cloves garlic, peeled
3 slices ginger, peeled
3 green onions, cut into 2" pieces
4 tablespoons wine
2 tablespoons light soy
  sauce
2 tablespoons hoisin sauce
2 tablespoons chili sauce
  or chili garlic sauce
1/2 teaspoon salt
1/4 teaspoon pepper

Insert steel blade. With machine running, drop garlic and ginger through the feed tube. Mince. Add remaining ingredients, except for pork and honey, blend. Marinate pork in this sauce for 2 hours, turning frequently. Reserve marinade. Brush the pork with honey. Place pork on rack in roasting pan, roast for 35 minutes at 350°.

Cool and slice the roast, basting with the sauce from the roasting pan.

Make extra pork to keep in freezer so you will have a supply for egg rolls, noodle dishes and garnishing. Serve hot, cool or accompanied by the basting sauce.

Makes 4 servings.

Chicken with Sesame Seeds

2 large chicken breasts
1/2 small head iceberg lettuce,
    cut into wedges
4 large green onions, cut
    in 2" lengths
2 tablespoons toasted
    sesame seeds

Sauce

1/2 cup roasted peanuts
2 tablespoons oyster sauce
1 teaspoon sesame oil
1 teaspoon sugar
1/2 teaspoon salt
2 tablespoons dark soy
    sauce
1 tablespoon cider vinegar

Simmer the chicken gently in water for 15 minutes and cool. Remove skin, slice into 1 1/2" by 1/4" strips.

Insert steel blade. Coarsely chop peanuts, using ON/OFF motion. Add sauce ingredients and blend. Marinate chicken in sauce for 1/2 hour. Drain.

Insert slicing disk. Shred lettuce. Place green onions in feed tube horizontally and slice. Toss onion and lettuce together with chicken. Sprinkle with sesame seeds, serve.

Makes 4 servings.

Chinese Almond Cookies

1/2 cup blanched almonds
1 cup shortening (1/2 lard and 1/2 butter)
1 cup sugar
1/2 teaspoon salt
1 teaspoon almond extract
2 jumbo eggs, separated
2 2/3 cup flour
1-3 oz. package whole blanched almonds

Preheat oven to 350°.

Insert steel blade. Mince 1/2 cup blanched almonds. Add shortening, sugar and cream. Add the salt, almond extract, 2 egg yolks, flour, and mix until blended. Chill the dough in the refrigerator for about 2 hours. Shape into 1 inch balls and dip the top of each cookie into the slightly beaten egg whites. Place on an ungreased cookie sheet. Press one almond on top of each cookie. Bake for 15 to 20 minutes. These cookies are the perfect compliment to a fresh fruit platter of oranges, strawberries and grapes.

Makes about 4 dozen cookies.

July: Asian Cabana Party

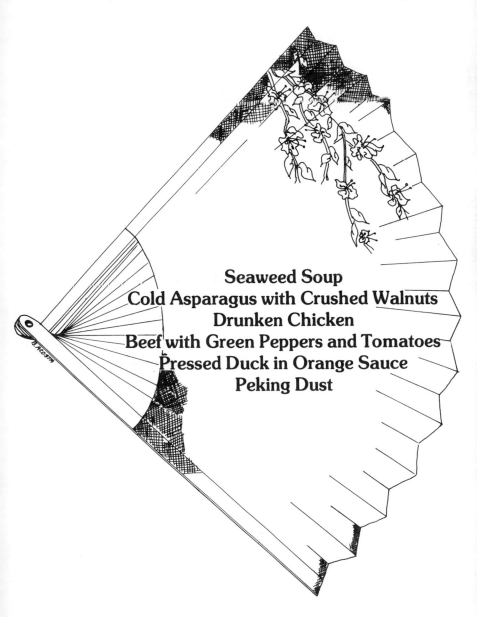

Seaweed Soup
Cold Asparagus with Crushed Walnuts
Drunken Chicken
Beef with Green Peppers and Tomatoes
Pressed Duck in Orange Sauce
Peking Dust

This is a perfect summer meal—easy to prepare and light. The varied textures and flavors combine and compliment each other so that the end result is sumptuous dining.

Seaweed Soup

1 *whole chicken breast, boned, skinned, partially frozen*
2 *green onions, cut in 2" pieces*
4 *cups chicken broth*
1/2 *sheet of seaweed*
1 *tablespoon sesame oil*
1/4 *pound cooked shrimp*

Insert slicing blade. Slice chicken. Set aside.

Insert steel blade. Chop green onions using ON/OFF motion.

Place chicken broth in large saucepan. Add sliced chicken, green onion and seaweed torn into small pieces. Simmer for 15 minutes. Add oil and simmer 5 minutes longer. Place shrimp in individual bowls, add soup. Serve hot.

Makes 8 servings.

Cold Asparagus
with Crushed Walnuts

*1 lb. fresh asparagus, discard woody ends and
  cut into 2" pieces*
10 walnuts shelled
5 tablespoons sugar
3 tablespoons rice vinegar
3 tablespoons light soy sauce
1/4 teaspoon fresh ground pepper

Cook asparagus in salted water until just tender. Drain and chill.

Insert steel blade. Chop walnuts. Add sugar, vinegar and soy sauce. Combine.

Gently toss the walnut dressing with the asparagus. Arrange on small individual dishes. Sprinkle with pepper.

Makes 6 servings.

Drunken Chicken

1-2 1/2 lb. chicken, cut into 8 pieces
2 cloves garlic, peeled
2 slices ginger, peeled
4 tablespoons oil

Sauce
1/2 cup light soy sauce
1 tablespoon sugar
1/2 teaspoon salt
1/8 teaspoon pepper
2 cups white wine

Insert steel blade. With machine running drop garlic and ginger through the feed tube and mince.

Combine sauce ingredients.

Heat oil in large heavy skillet and brown chicken. Add sauce. Simmer for 45 minutes, covered. Serve hot with rice.

Makes 4 servings.

Beef with Green Peppers and Tomatoes

1 lb. flank steak, partially frozen
2 cloves garlic, peeled
1 teaspoon salted black beans, washed and mashed
1/2 teaspoon salt
1 teaspoon sherry
2 large bell peppers, seeded and halved lengthwise
2 large tomatoes, cut into quarters
2 tablespoons oil

Sauce

4 teaspoons light soy sauce
1/2 teaspoon sugar
1 tablespoon cornstarch
1 tablespoon water

Insert slicing blade. Cut meat into pieces that fit into feed tube. Slice each piece, using firm pressure.

Insert steel blade. With the machine running drop garlic through the feed tube, mince. Heat oil in wok or heavy skillet. Add garlic, black beans and salt. Stir-fry for 30 seconds. Add beef and sherry. Stir-fry until beef changes color.

Insert slicing disk. Slice peppers with medium pressure. Add peppers, tomatoes, and sauce to wok. Stir-fry until sauce begins to thicken. Serve hot with rice.

Makes 4 servings.

Pressed Duck in Orange Sauce

1-5 lb. duck

1 egg white
1/3 cup water chestnut powder
*   or cornstarch*
3 cups peanut oil

Seasoning

2 slices ginger, peeled
2 teaspoons five spice powder
1 tablespoon salt
1/4 cup sherry

Thickening

1 tablespoon cornstarch
1 tablespoon water

Garnish

1/4 cup sliced almonds
kumquats
parsley

Orange Sauce

2 slices ginger, peeled
1 tablespoon sherry
2 teaspoons white vinegar
1 teaspoon dark soy sauce
4 teaspoons sugar
juice from 1 orange
1/2 cup clear chicken broth
2 tablespoons Grand Marnier liqueur
2 tablespoons plum sauce

Place 3 quarts water in wok, add seasoning and bring to a rapid boil. Lower duck carefully into broth. Cover wok, lower heat to medium and cook for 1 hour. Gently remove duck to a flat surface, cool. Dry with paper toweling.

Brush egg white evenly on the duck. Then generously sprinkle water chestnut powder over duck. Steam duck on rack over water for 20 minutes. Place duck on a rack to dry and cool. Remove breastbone and backbone from duck leaving wings and drumsticks intact. Work gently so that the duck will not be torn. Cut duck into quarters.

Insert steel blade. With machine running, drop ginger through the feed tube, mince. Add remaining sauce ingredients and blend.

Heat sauce over medium heat in small saucepan for 1 minute. Add cornstarch mixed with water, stir until sauce begins to thicken. Keep warm.

Heat oil in wok until hot. Deep fry duck maintaining high heat until both sides are golden brown, about 10 minutes. Remove to chopping board and drain. Cut into 1" x 3" pieces. Place on serving platter. Pour sauce over duck. Top with almonds. Garnish with kumquats and parsley.

Makes 4 servings.

Peking Dust

1 large can (15½ oz.) chestnut puree
3 tablespoons brown sugar
1 cup pecans
1/2 cup granulated sugar
1 cup heavy cream
3 tablespoons granulated sugar
10 maraschino cherries

Insert steel blade. Mix chestnut puree with brown sugar. Set aside. Place pecans in boiling water for one minute and then drain.

Insert steel blade. Add 1/2 cup sugar and pecans to work bowl and chop using ON/OFF motion. Chill bowl, steel blade and cream. Whip cream with 3 tablespoons sugar. (This takes about 10 minutes). Place in large mixing bowl and fold chestnut mixture into the heavy cream. Divide into chilled serving cups. Top with pecans (dust), add a cherry or candied strawberry. Heavenly.

Makes 10 small servings.

August: The Gathering

Great Wall Chicken Soup
Saucy Butterfly Shrimp with Walnuts
Chicken Szechuan
Fresh Coconut Ice Cream

The unusual fare creates the perfect mood for dining amongst good friends—a Friday night bridge party, a summer luncheon or a teeanger's birthday party. The Chicken Szechuan could even be prepared at the table by host, hostess or even one of the guests!

Great Wall Chicken Soup

4 cups chicken stock
1/3 lb. raw pork, cut into 1/2" cubes
1/3 lb. firm raw fish, cut into 1/2" cubes
2 tablespoons cornstarch
1 extra large egg
1/4 teaspoon salt
3 green onions, cut into 2" pieces

   Insert steel blade. Place pork, fish, cornstarch, egg and salt in bowl. Mince with ON/OFF motion. Remove to medium-sized mixing bowl.

   Insert slicing blade. Slice onions lengthwise.

   Heat stock to a boil. Drop fish mixture from teaspoon into soup. Simmer for 10 minutes. Garnish with onions.

   Makes 6 servings.

Saucy Butterfly Shrimp with Walnuts

1/2 cup walnuts
1/2 medium head lettuce, cut into wedges
18 large shrimp, peeled and deveined
2 cups peanut oil
5 pieces bacon, each cut into 4 pieces

Batter

2 green onions, cut into 2" pieces
1/2 cup flour
1/4 cup water
2 eggs, lightly beaten
1 teaspoon sherry

Sweet Sauce

1/2 cup wine vinegar
1/2 cup sugar
1/4 cup pineapple juice
5 tablespoons catsup
1/2 teaspoon salt
2 teaspoons cornstarch mixed with 2 tablespoons water

Insert steel blade. Chop nuts using ON/OFF motion.

Insert slicing disk. Slice lettuce. Arrange on serving plate.

Insert steel blade. Chop green onions. Add remaining batter ingredients and mix until combined.

Insert plastic blade. Mix all ingredients except cornstarch until combined. In small saucepan heat sauce. When it starts to boil, add cornstarch and simmer until mixture begins to thicken. Keep warm.

Cut almost through the shrimp (lengthwise) and flatten. Pat shrimp dry with paper toweling. Wrap each shrimp in a piece of bacon. Heat oil in heavy skillet to 380°. Dip in batter and fry. Cook until golden brown. Turn and cook other side. Remove with slotted spoon. Drain on a paper toweling. Place shrimp on lettuce. Pour warmed sauce over. Sprinkle chopped walnuts over sauce. Serve hot shrimp with rice. Makes 4 servings.

Chicken Szechuan ✓

2 chicken breasts, boned, skinned, partially frozen
1 egg white
1 tablespoons cornstarch
4 tablespoons peanut oil
1 tablespoon red pepper flakes
1 cup dry roasted peanuts
3 green onions, cut into 2" pieces

Sauce

1 tablespoon wine
1 teaspoon sugar
4 tablespoon light soy sauce

Insert slicing disk. Slice chicken breats. Combine egg white and cornstarch, mix with sliced chicken.

Heat oil in wok or in heavy skillet. Stir-fry hot pepper flakes for 10 seconds. Add chicken and stir-fry until chicken turns color. Combine ingredients for sauce in small bowl. Stir sauce into chicken. Add peanuts and mix well. Remove chicken to serving plate.

Insert slicing disk. Slice green onions. Garnish chicken with green onions. Serve hot with rice or noodles.

Makes 4 servings.

Fresh Coconut Ice Cream

1 medium coconut
2 cups warm milk
1/2 teaspoon vanilla extract
cherries for topping

Syrup
3/4 cup water
3/4 cup sugar
1/8 teaspoon cream
      of tartar

Make sure that coconut is full of liquid. Make holes in two eyes of the coconut. Drain liquid and reserve. Split shell. Remove outer skin of the coconut. Cut meat of the coconut into cubes.

Insert grating blade. Process coconut. Measure 2 cups of coconut. Reserve one cup for topping.

Insert steel blade. Add one cup of the coconut and one cup of the warm milk. Process for 10 seconds. Remove to bowl. Combine with second cup of warm milk.

Using a small saucepan combine syrup ingredients. Bring to a boil and boil 3 minutes, stirring often. Cool.

Combine coconut milk, syrup and vanilla. Place in shallow bowl. Freeze for 4 hours, stirring twice during this time.

Top with reserved coconut and cherries.

Makes 1 quart.

September: Fall Celebration

Far East Stuffed Mushrooms
Szechuan Bean Curd
Orange Flavored Beef
Cantonese Pheasant
Gingered Papaya

Pheasant is a delicacy in America or the Orient. If you can't find the rare bird, substitute cornish hens. This meal is marvelous in the fall when spicier foods are more appealing. You can decorate the table with plummage and chrysanthemums.

Far East Stuffed Mushrooms

20 large dried mushrooms
1/2 cup dry sherry
1/4 lb. lean pork, cut into 1" chunks
1/4 lb. uncooked shrimp, washed and deveined
6 water chestnuts
1 egg white
1 tablespoon cornstarch

Sauce
2 green onions, cut into 2" lengths
6 tablespoons light soy sauce
2 tablespoons dry sherry

Clean mushrooms and remove stems. Place mushrooms in a large bowl, cover with hot water, add sherry. Soak for 3 hours. Squeeze mushrooms dry.

Inert steel blade. Process pork and shrimp using ON/OFF motion until minced. Add water chestnuts, egg white, and cornstarch. Process with ON/OFF motion until minced. Stuff mushroom caps with pork and shrimp mixture. Steam for 35 to 40 minutes.

Insert steel blade. Mince green onions. Add soy sauce and sherry to onion. Heat sauce for 1 minute in small saucepan. Drizzle over mushrooms before serving.

Makes 10 appetizer servings.

Szechuan Bean Curd

1 clove garlic, peeled
2 stalks green onions, cut into 2" pieces
4 ounces pork (or beef), cut into 1" pieces
2 cup peanut oil
1 cup bean curd*, cut into 1/2" pieces

Thickening

2 tablespoons cornstarch
2 teaspoons cold water

Sauce

1 tablespoon hot bean paste
2 tablespoons light soy sauce
1 teaspoon salt
2/3 cups chicken soup stock

Combine

1 teaspoon sesame oil

Insert steel blade. With the machine running, drop the garlic through the feed tube and process until minced. Set aside. Add the green onion and chop. Set aside.

Chop pork with ON/OFF motion.

Using a small bowl make a paste with the cornstarch and water. Heat peanut oil in wok or heavy skillet to 380 degrees. Fry bean curd for 30 seconds (or boil in water). Remove all oil except 3 tablespoons. Reheat the wok and fry the chopped pork, add garlic and sauce. Combine and simmer for 3 minutes.

Add the cornstarch paste and stir-fry for 30 seconds or until sauce thickens. Sprinkle with reserved green onions and sesame oil. Place in a bowl and serve with rice.

This traditional dish is cooked with very little liquid so that the bean curd absorbs all the exciting flavors.

Makes 4 servings.

*Bean curd is found in the produce department of some supermarkets and in Chinese grocery stores.

Orange Flavored Beef

1 lb. flank steak,
   partially frozen
1 slice ginger root, peeled
2 cloves garlic, peeled
3 green onions, cut into
   1 1/2" lengths
rind from one orange
2 teaspoons sherry
2 cups peanut oil

Marinade

2 teaspoons dark soy sauce
2 teaspoons sherry
1 tablespoon cornstarch
1 1/2 teaspoons oyster sauce

Sauce

1 teaspoon dark soy sauce
2 teaspoons wine vinegar
1/2 teaspoon cornstarch
1 teaspoon water

Insert slicing blade. Wedge each piece of steak in the feed tube and slice using heavy pressure. Place in a mixing bowl. Combine marinade ingredients and pour over meat. Let stand 20 minutes.

Insert steel blade. With machine running, drop in the ginger, garlic, green onion, and orange peel. Continue processing until they are finely chopped. Set aside. Heat oil in wok over high heat. Add beef, stir to separate pieces. Blanch until the beef loses its red color. Remove to a medium bowl.

Insert plastic blade. Mix sauce ingredients in the work bowl. Set aside.

Carefully remove all but 3 tablespoons of oil from the wok. Heat oil, then add the orange peel mixture, stir-fry for 30 seconds. Return beef to wok, splash in sherry and mix well. Stir in sauce mixture and stir-fry until sauce is thickened. Serve hot with rice.

Makes 4 servings.

Cantonese Pheasant

1 leek, cleaned
1 cup Chinese mushrooms
rind of 1 orange
1 slice ginger root, peeled
5 tablespoons peanut oil
1-2 1/2 to 3 lb. pheasant,
    cleaned, cut into quarters
1/4 teaspoon salt
1/8 teaspoon pepper
1 teaspoon rosemary
1/4 cup dry white wine
2 tablespoons dark soy sauce
2 cups water

Insert slicing disk. Using medium pressure slice leek, set aside. Soak mushrooms in hot water for 30 minutes, cut off woody stems, drain.

Insert slicing disk. Slice mushrooms using heavy pressure. Set aside.

Insert steel blade. With machine running drop in orange peel and ginger, mince. Heat oil in heavy skillet, add pheasant to skillet skin side down. Brown well on both sides, sprinkle with salt and pepper. Add mushrooms, leek, orange peel, ginger, rosemary, wine and soy sauce. Add 2 cups of water to the skillet. Bring to a boil, lower heat to simmer, cover and cook until tender, about 2 hours. Remove pheasant to a warm serving platter, cover with cooking sauce and serve with rice.

Makes 4 servings.

Gingered Papaya

2 slices ginger, peeled
2 papayas, ripe but firm
4 tablespoons butter
2 tablespoons lime juice

Insert steel blade. With machine running drop ginger through the feed tube and process until minced. Cut the papayas lengthwise and scoop out the seeds. Arrange the halves in a greased baking dish. Melt together the butter, lime juice, and the ginger. Spoon ginger mixture into the cavity of each papaya.

Bake in a 350° oven for 30 minutes, basting occasionally. Serve hot.

Makes 4 servings.

October: Oriental Block Party

Winter Melon Soup
Molded Sausage and Rice
Sweet and Sour Fish
Chicken with Green Peppers
Glazed Bananas

The focal point of this fall fantasy meal is the soup—delicate yet dramatic in a tureen carved from a whole melon. It is pleasing to the eyes as well as the palate. The other dishes each dramatic in its own way, add to the festive mood created by the soup.

Winter Melon Soup

1 lb. winter melon* (Buy a 1/2 melon if you are
planning to serve in it.)
6 Chinese mushrooms
4 cups chicken stock
1/2 teaspoon sugar
1/2 teaspoon salt
1/8 teaspoon white pepper
1/2 teaspoon cornstarch

Scrape flesh of melon from skin leaving a firm shell.

Insert slicing blade. Slice the winter melon. Set aside. Soak mushrooms in 1 cup hot water for 15 minutes or until soft. Remove stems. With heavy pressure slice mushrooms in the food processor. Place chicken stock in medium saucepan and simmer for 4 minutes. Add remaining ingredients. Simmer for 15 minutes. Check for seasoning. Pour into a winter melon shell and serve.

This soup makes a dramatic presentation. To enhance the drama you can shape the upper edge of the melon in a zig-zag design and then carve a design perhaps a dragon breathing fire on the outside of the melon.

Garnish with Smithfield ham if available.

Makes 6-8 servings.

*Winter melon can be obtained in the fall. It's worth waiting for! It is available in Oriental food markets.

Molded Sausage and Rice

5 Chinese sausages *
1 3/4 cup water
1 cup uncooked rice, washed
1/2 teaspoon salt
1 teaspoon peanut oil
1 small can green peas

Insert slicing blade. Slice the sausages using heavy pressure. Place water in medium saucepan, add rice, salt and peanut oil. Heat until it reaches a rapid boil, stir occasionally.

Add sausages to the pan of rice. Cover with a tight fitting lid and shut off heat. In 20 minutes rice will be cooked. Unmold on heated plate and decorate with green peas. Makes 3-4 servings.

*Chinese sausages can be purchased from a Chinese grocery store.

Sweet and Sour Fish

1 *whole red snapper or bass, 1 1/2 pounds, cleaned
and scaled (leaving head and tail intact)*
2 *teaspoons salt*
1/2 *cup all-purpose flour*
3 *cups peanut oil*

Sweet and Sour Sauce

1 *tablespoon cornstarch*
1/2 *cup brown sugar*
8 *tablespoons pineapple juice*
2 *teaspoons light soy sauce*
1/3 *cup vinegar*

Cut 5 slits diagonally on each side of the fish. Rub
fish with salt, rinse. Dust fish with flour. Heat oil to 380°
or until bubbles form on a wooden chopstick. Deep fry
the fish until it is brown and crisp or about 6 minutes.
Keep warm in oven at 300° until ready to assemble.
Serve with Sweet and Sour Sauce.

Insert plastic blade. Add cornstarch and brown
sugar. Use ON/OFF motion for 3 seconds. Add remaining ingredients and process just until well mixed.
Heat sauce in a small saucepan until slightly thickened.

Makes 4 servings.

Chicken with Green Peppers and Peanuts

8 oz. boned chicken
  breasts
1 green pepper, seeded,
  halved with tops and
  bottoms cut straight
  across
8 tablespoons peanut oil
3 tablespoons unsalted
  roasted peanuts
4 ounces bamboo shoots
1 clove garlic, peeled
1 slice ginger, peeled
3 green onions
1 teaspoon crushed
  chili pepper

Marinade
1 small egg white
1 teaspoon cornstarch
1/4 teaspoon salt
1/8 teaspoon pepper

Sauce
1 1/2 tablespoons light
  soy sauce
1 teaspoon sherry
1/2 teaspoon sugar

Partially freeze chicken until you can just insert a fork into it.

Insert slicing disk. Slice chicken. Mix marinade ingredients in a medium-sized mixing bowl. Add sliced chicken. Set aside.

Insert slicing disk. Use light pressure and slice green pepper. Heat 4 tablespoons oil in wok or heavy skillet and fry peanuts over medium heat, being careful not to let them burn. Remove to a plate. Add the bamboo shoots and pepper. Cook 30 seconds. Remove and wipe out the wok.

Insert steel blade. With machine running, drop the garlic, ginger and green onion through the feed tube. Process until minced. Heat remaining 4 tablespoons oil in wok. Add garlic mixture and chili pepper. Stir fry for 30 seconds. Add chicken and stir-fry until chicken is cooked. Add bamboo shoots and pepper and mix well. Mix sauce ingredients together, add to wok, stir to combine. Stir in peanuts. Serve hot with rice.

Makes 4 servings.

111

Glazed Bananas

1/3 cup walnuts
3 firm bananas, sliced in 3" long wedges
2 extra large eggs, slightly beaten
1/2 cup cornstarch
3 cups peanut oil
1 cup sugar
1/4 cup water
3 tablespoons oil
1 large bowl with cold water and ice cubes

Insert steel blade. Place walnuts in bowl. Chop nuts with 5 ON/OFF turns. Set aside.

Dip bananas in eggs and roll in the cornstarch. Set aside. Coat serving dish with 1 tablespoon of oil. Heat 3 cups oil to 380° and deep fry bananas until golden brown. Remove from wok with strainer, drain and keep warm in a 300 degree oven. While frying bananas, heat sugar, water and 3 tablespoons oil to hard ball stage on candy thermometer, or until a long thread spins from the end of a chopstick.

Quickly coat each banana with syrup, then dip in bowl of ice and water. Remove to an oiled plate. Enjoy!

November: Asian Fondue For Good Friends

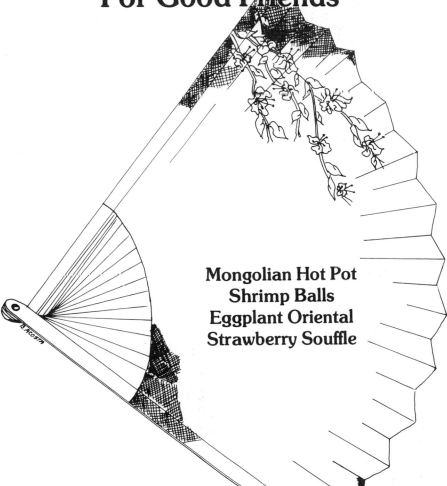

**Mongolian Hot Pot
Shrimp Balls
Eggplant Oriental
Strawberry Souffle**

A mongolian hot pot is a Chinese version of the fondue. Although a festive dish now, at first it was considered quite ordinary. Some say it was introduced by nomadic mongol lords who overran northern China in the Thirteenth Century. Those invaders would set great cauldrons of water to boil over the fire, drop slivers of mutton into the water until they were cooked, and then season it. They would end the meal with the broth which had become a rich, flavorful soup. This is a gourmet favorite for entertaining, and an added benefit is all the ingredients are low calorie.

Mongolian Hot Pot

A hot pot is the ultimate in Chinese conviviality. Guests surround a hot pot each cooking his own meal in the bubbling brew thus helping to improve the flavor of the broth. Ideally a Chinese hot pot utensil should be used, in which case 5 charcoal briquettes are needed for the center chimney. Fortunately, however, a fondue pot or electric skillet works quite well.

All ingredients are sliced wafer-thin and arranged attractively on serving platters which surround the hot pot. Each guest should be armed with a plate, a wire ladle, slotted spoon or chopsticks, a good supply of rice as well as a soup bowl for the meal's grand finale—a bowl of well-flavored broth. Sherry may be passed so that each guest may further enhance his broth.

Any hot pot lends itself to substitutions and changes. Just be certain when making changes that you have included enough food for the number of guests you are serving. This particular hot pot serves 10.

The order of cooking of the food is optional. However it is best to cook meat before fish and both should be cooked before the vegetables as the meat and fish tend to flavor the broth. Each guest cooks food to his taste, dips it in a sauce, and devours!

INGREDIENTS

4 cups chicken stock
1 pound chicken breast,
  partially frozen
1 pound flank steak,
  partially frozen
1/2 pound shrimp
1/2 pound oysters
8 green onions, cut
  in 2" pieces
2 ounces bean thread
hot cooked rice

1 pound fresh spinach,
  washed well
2 cups bean curd cubes
1/2 pound Chinese
    mushrooms, soaked
1 can bamboo shoots
1/3 pound snow peas

Garnish
parsley
green pepper
tomatoes

Insert slicing disk. Slice chicken. Set aside. Slice meat. Set aside. Slice green onions by placing them horizontally in feed tube. Set aside. Slice Chinese mushrooms. Set aside.

Boil bean threads for 2 minutes in hot water and drain. Cut in 3" lengths. Place on a platter and decorate with green onions.

Separate leaves of washed spinach. Arrange on two platters and place cleaned, shelled and deveined shrimp on top.

Arrange meat, vegetables and remaining ingredients attractively on platters.

Place hot soup in pot which is surrounded by platters of food, sauces and rice.

SAUCES:

Mild Egg Sauce

1 cup light soy sauce
2 tablespoons vinegar
4 eggs

Insert plastic blade. Add ingredients to work bowl. Process until smooth.

Hot Mustard Sauce

1/2 cup dry mustard
1 tablespoon oil
1/2 cup boiling water
1/2 cup white wine
1/4 teaspoon salt

Add salt to the boiling water, then add mustard. Add oil and wine. Let stand 30 minutes before serving.

Hoisin Sauce

12 tablespoons hoisin sauce
1 tablespoon sesame oil
1 teaspoon sugar

Heat ingredients in a small saucepan to boiling point. Mix. Remove from heat. Cool and serve.

Shrimp Balls

1 slice ginger, peeled
2 tablespoons pork fat
1/3 cup water chestnuts
1 pound fresh shrimp deveined, cleaned or 3/4
  pound peeled frozen shrimp
1/8 teaspoon white pepper
1/2 teaspoon salt
1 teaspoon sesame oil
1 teaspoon cornstarch
1 egg white, beaten lightly

3 cups peanut oil

Insert steel blade. With machine running, drop ginger through the feed tube, mince. Leave steel blade in place. Add pork fat and process until minced. Add water chestnuts and shrimp. Turn machine ON/OFF until you have a smooth paste. Add the white pepper, salt, sesame oil, and cornstarch, blend. Remove to a bowl, add beaten egg white, blend.

Preheat oven to 250°.

Heat oil to 380° in wok or heavy skillet. Slide shrimp mixture by teaspoonfuls carefully into the oil. Turn balls so they will cook evenly. Repeat until you have 6 shrimp balls in oil. Fry until they are golden brown, about 1 minute. Drain and put them in the warm oven until the other are cooked. Serve them hot.

Makes 20 shrimp balls.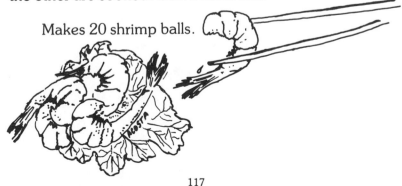

Eggplant Oriental

1 pound eggplant

2 cloves garlic
4 tablespoons peanut oil
1/4 teaspoon salt

2 tablespoons wine
6 tablespoons chicken stock
1 tablespoon oyster sauce
1 teaspoon light soy sauce
1/2 teaspoon sesame oil

Remove skin from the eggplant. Cut in quarters lengthwise, in shapes that will fit the feed tube.

Insert slicing disk. Slice eggplant with medium pressure, set aside.

Insert steel blade. With machine running, drop garlic through the feed tube, mince. Heat peanut oil in wok. When oil is hot, add garlic and salt. Stir fry about 15 seconds, until garlic has turned a golden brown. Add eggplant and stir to coat. Add wine, chicken stock and cover. Cook one minute. Add oyster sauce, soy sauce and sesame oil. Stir-fry about 30 seconds (only until eggplant is soft.) Serve hot.

Makes 4 servings.

Strawberry Souffle

3 cups strawberries washed and hulled
6 extra large eggs, separated
1 cup sugar
1/2 cup orange liqueur
1 cup heavy cream
1 cup sugar
1/3 cup orange juice

Garnish
1/2 cup heavy cream, whipped
8 large whole strawberries

Insert steel blade. Puree strawberries. Set aside. Wash bowl. **Reinsert steel blade.** Add egg yolks and beat until thick and lemon colored. Add 1 cup sugar and beat until dissolved. Stir in 1/2 cup strawberry puree. Place in top of double boiler and cook over hot water about 10 minutes until thickened. Stir frequently, cool. Add orange liqueur slowly until thoroughly mixed.

Combine 1 cup sugar and orange juice in medium saucepan. Cook uncovered over medium heat, stirring until dissolved. Continue cooking for 5 minutes. Cool.

With mixer beat egg whites until soft peaks form. Very slowly fold in cooled orange syrup. Continue beating for 2 minutes.

With mixer whip cream. Fold into cooked yolk mixture. Fold in remaining strawberry puree. Gently fold in egg whites.

Lightly oil a 1 1/2 qt. souffle dish. Pour mixture into dish. Chill 3 hours or until set. To serve remove collar. Garnish top with whipped cream and strawberries.

Makes 10-12 servings.

December: A Dim Sum Brunch

Green Onion Pancake
Fried Chicken in Paper
Stuffed Sweet Peppers
Fried Pot Stickers Dumplings
Egg Rolls
Sweet Sauce
Sherry Butter Cookies
Orange Freeze

A Dim Sum is the Chinese version of an American brunch. Guests are invited for 1:00 P.M. Everyone enjoys wine or champagne, and Chinese finger foods or as the Chinese call them, Dim Sum.

Green Onion Pancake

3 green onions, cut into 2" lengths
2 cups all purpose flour, unsifted
1/2 teaspoon baking powder
3/4 cup boiling water
3 tablespoons vegetable shortening
Kosher salt (coarse)

1 cup peanut oil

Insert steel blade. Chop green onions. Set aside.

Insert steel blade. Place flour and baking powder in bowl. With machine running pour water through feed tube. Mix until dough ball forms. Place in a greased bowl, cover. Let rest at room temperature for a least 2 hours. The dough may be sticky.

Using a lightly floured board, divide dough into 2 equal portions and knead each piece for one minute. With a rolling pin, roll each ball into a pancake. Spread with 1 1/2 tablespoons of shortening, sprinkle with chopped green onions and sprinkle with salt. Roll up the pancake in jelly roll fashion.

Wind each pancake into circular shape, starting at the center and coiling around until dough is used up. Roll out with rolling pin to a 10 inch round shape. Heat 1/2 cup oil in large skillet. Pan fry pancakes, one at a time, over medium heat. Turn once so that both sides are golden brown. Cut into large slices. Serve at once. Cut with scissors into 8 wedges. Freezes well before frying.

Makes two 10" breads.

Fried Chicken in Paper

1 chicken breast,
  partially frozen
2 green onions
  cut into 2" lengths
1 green pepper, halved
6 dried mushrooms
4 tablespoons sesame oil
4 pieces rice paper or wax
  paper, cut into 8" squares
3 cups peanut oil

Marinade
2 slices ginger, peeled
1/4 teaspoon salt
1/4 teaspoon pepper
1/4 teaspoon garlic powder
2 teaspoons white wine
1/2 teaspoon cinnamon

Garnish
shredded lettuce
cherry tomatoes

Insert slicing disk. Slice chicken. Set aside.

Insert slicing blade. Slice green onions. Slice green pepper. Soak mushrooms in hot water for 15 minutes, break off stems and squeeze dry. Slice using heavy pressure.

Combine marinade ingredients in mixing bowl.

Insert steel blade. With machine running drop ginger through the feed tube and mince. Add to marinade. Combine chicken with marinade and let stand 20 minutes.

Rub one side of paper with sesame oil. Drain chicken. Place 1 strip of pepper, 1/2 teaspoon green onion, 1 mushroom strip and 3 small chicken slices on the center of the paper. Fold in envelope style and seal tightly with water.

Heat oil in wok or heavy skillet to 380°. Fry envelopes in oil, five at a time for 30 seconds, turn over and cook for another 15 seconds; or until chicken changes color. Remove with slotted spoon. Drain on paper towels.

These packages look lovely placed unopened on shredded lettuce with small tomatoes in the center of the platter. They may be made early in the day and fried just before serving. Serve warm.

Makes 12 chicken packages.

Stuffed Sweet Peppers

2 slice ginger, peeled
6 oz. pork, cut into 1/2" pieces, chilled
1 green onion, cut into 1" piece
2 oz. water chestnuts
2 tablespoons sherry
1 1/2 tablespoons light soy sauce
1/4 teaspoon salt
3 sweet red or green peppers, seeded, and
   quartered lengthwise
4 teaspoons cornstarch
4 tablespoons oil
1 teaspoon sugar
3 tablespoons light soy sauce
1/2 cup water

Insert steel blade. With machine running drop ginger through the feed tube and mince. Add pork, onion, water chestnuts, sherry, 1 1/2 tablespoons soy sauce and salt to bowl. Mince with ON/OFF motion until meat is finely chopped.

Stuff peppers with mixture. Sprinkle tops with cornstarch. Heat oil in large heavy skillet. Place peppers in skillet, meat side down and fry for 2 minutes. Combine sugar, soy sauce and water. Add to skillet. Cover and cook for 10 minutes or until pork is well cooked.

Remove and invert peppers with a spatula, so that the pork side is up. Serve hot.

Makes 12 pieces of stuffed peppers.

Fried Pot Sticker Dumplings

Dough

2 1/2 cups flour
1 cup cold water

Filling

5 ounces pork, chilled and cut into 1/2" pieces
3 green onions, cut in 2" lengths
1/2 teaspoon sesame oil
1/4 cup bamboo shoots
1 1/2 teaspoon light soy sauce
1/2 teaspoon wine
1/8 teaspoon pepper
6 tablespoons peanut oil
1 cup hot water

Sauce

2 tablespoons light soy sauce
1 teaspoon vinegar

Insert steel blade. Place flour in machine. With machine running pour hot water through the feed tube. Pour cold water through the feed tube. Process only until dough ball forms. Place in medium bowl for 15 minutes, covered.

Insert steel blade. Chop pork with ON/OFF motion. Add green onions, sesame oil, bamboo shoots, soy sauce, wine and pepper to bowl. Mince filling with ON/OFF motion.

Roll out dough on lightly floured board to 1/8" thickness. Cut with a 2 1/2" cookie cutter, filled with 1 teaspoon filling. Seal edges with a twisting motion, into a half moon shape.

Place 6 tablespoons oil in hot skillet. Place pot stickers in skillet and fry until lightly brown on one side. Pour water over pot stickers. Cover quickly and steam for 10 minutes. Serve hot with sauce.

Makes 30 dumplings.

Egg Rolls

1/2 pound small shrimp
   washed, deveined
2 large carrots
2 cloves garlic, peeled
3 green onions;
   cut in 2" pieces
5 dried mushrooms
1 cup bamboo shoots
2 cups lettuce
3 cups peanut oil
1 egg slightly beaten
1 pound egg roll wrappers

Marinade
3 teaspoons white wine
1/4 teaspoon salt
1 teaspoon cornstarch

Sauce
4 tablespoons light soy
  sauce
1 tablespoons cornstarch

Combine marinade ingredients and marinate shrimp for 20 minutes, Drain.

Insert shredding disk. Shred carrots and set aside.

Insert steel blade. With machine running, drop the garlic and green onions through the feed tube and mince.

Insert slicng disk. Soak mushrooms in hot water for 15 minutes, Drain. Discard tough ends. Slice. Slice bamboo shoots and lettuce. Heat 1 teaspoon oil in wok or heavy skillet. Add garlic and green onions. Stir-fry until golden brown. Add shrimps and stir-fry until cooked. Remove to bowl. Heat 2 tablespoons oil in wok and add carrots. Stir-fry for 15 seconds. Add bamboo shoots and stir-fry to combine. Add mushrooms and lettuce. Combine and stir-fry for 30 seconds. Combine with shrimp and sauce. Cool.

Place 2 tablespoons filling on one egg roll wrapper. Seal with egg in envelope style. Place the sealed side down on lightly floured cookie sheet until they have all been rolled.

Heat peanut oil to 380° and deep fry egg rolls, three at a time, until they are golden brown. Drain on paper toweling. Serve with sweet sauce and hot mustard.

Makes 20 large egg rolls.

Sweet Sauce

1 large jar of apricot jam (12 oz.)
3 tablespoons white vinegar
3 tablespoons water
1 small jar minced pimento (2 oz.)

Insert plastic blade. Add all ingredients and mix until blended using ON/OFF motion. Remove to medium size saucepan and heat to boiling point. Reduce heat to simmer. Continue simmering for one minute. Remove to serving dish. Cool and serve. Makes 1 3/4 cups sweet sauce.

Hot Sauce

2 tablespoons mustard powder
3 tablespoons wine or water

Mix mustard with enough water or wine to make a thin paste.

Sherry Butter Cookies

1 cup butter, chilled, cut into 1/2" chunks
1 cup sugar
1 extra large egg
1 tablespoon sherry
2 cups all-purpose flour
1 teaspoon baking powder

Insert steel blade. Combine butter and sugar with ON/OFF motion. Then let machine run until mixture is creamed. Place egg, sherry, flour and baking powder in work bowl. Process until combined. Drop by teaspoonfuls on a greased cookie sheet. Bake at 400° for 9 minutes. These are very simple delicious cookies, which are good served with fruit or ice cream.

Makes 36 cookies

Orange Freeze

1 pint vanilla ice cream
1 pint orange sherbet
1/4 cup Grand Marnier

Insert steel blade. Add ice cream, sherbet and Grand Marnier. Process until blended. Serve immediately in individual bowls or parfait glasses or keep in freezer until serving time.

Makes 6 servings.

December: "Helping Hands" Holiday Dinner

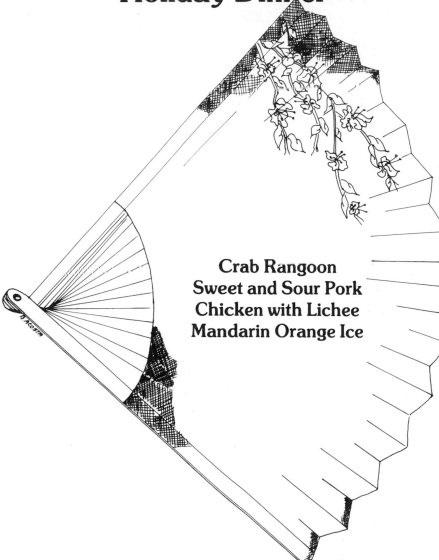

Crab Rangoon
Sweet and Sour Pork
Chicken with Lichee
Mandarin Orange Ice

This menu lends itself to having guests help with cooking—a perfect menu when houseguests abound. Noodles with hot sauce is exquisite. The noodles are shaped in a mound,—pyramid style—then covered with cucumbers and chicken. This is a substantial meal which makes excellent winter fare.

Crab Rangoon

1 clove garlic, peeled
1/2 pound cream cheese, cut into 1" cubes
1/2 pound crabmeat, remove shell
1/8 teaspoon Worchestershire sauce
1/2 teaspoon salt
1/4 teaspoon white pepper
1 package wonton wrappers
1 egg, slightly beaten
2 cups peanut oil for frying

Insert steel blade. With machine running drop in the garlic and process until finely minced. Stop the machine. Add cream cheese and turn the machine ON/OFF until the cheese is partially creamed. Add the carbmeat, Worchestershire sauce, salt and pepper. Process until the mixture is well blended.

Place 1/2 teaspoon of the filling in the center of each wonton wrapper. Fold each wrapper in half, use the egg as a binder to seal the edges. Fold in half again and pinch the edges.

Heat oil to 380°. Carefully lower wontons into the oil. Fry 5 at a time. Fry for 45 seconds or until golden brown. Drain on paper toweling. Serve with a plum sauce, which can be obtained ready made.

Makes about 35 wontons.

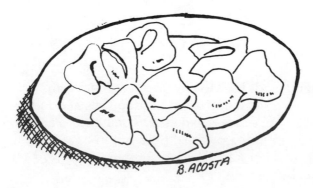

B. ACOSTA

Noodles with Hot Sauce

1 chicken breast, cooked, boned, skinned
1 large cucumber, peeled and seeded
2 green onions, cut in 2" lengths
2 extra large eggs scrambled
4 cups soup noodles or thin spaghetti, cooked and
  drained
2 tablespoons sesame oil

Sauce

1 tablespoon light soy sauce
1 tablespoon white wine
1 tablespoon vinegar
1/2 teaspoon sugar
1 teaspoon chili sauce
1 teaspoon salt
1/2 cup chicken soup stock

Insert slicing blade. Shred the chicken, set aside. Slice the cucumber with slicing disc, set aside.

Insert steel blade. With the steel blade in place chop the green onions with 3-4 ON/OFF turns.

Toss noodles with the sesame oil and onion, arrange on a heated plate.

Insert plastic blade. Add soy sauce, wine, vinegar, sugar, salt, chili sauce and soup stock to the work bowl, process until blended. Add sauce to noodles. Add chicken to noodles, then add cucumbers on top of chicken, top with scrambled eggs. Bring to table in pyramid. Then toss noodles when ready to eat. Serve warm or cold.

Makes 8 servings.

Sweet and Sour Pork

1 1/2 pounds lean pork,
    cubed
1/4 cup flour
2 cups peanut oil
1 large pepper
1 large tomato
3/4 cups canned pineapple
    chunks, drained

Sweet & Sour Sauce

1/2 cup sugar
1/2 cup vinegar
2 teaspoons light soy
    sauce
1/2 cup pineapple juice
3 tablespoons catsup

Batter

1 clove garlic, peeled
1/2 cup flour
1 extra large egg
1/4 cup water
1/2 teaspoon salt
1/4 teaspoon baking
    powder

Heat oil wok or heavy skillet to 380°.

Insert steel blade. With machine running, drop in the garlic and continue processing until finely minced. Add flour, egg, salt, water and baking powder. Turn the machine ON/OFF until mixed. Pour batter into a shallow dish and dip meat into this batter to coat evenly. Then lower a few pieces at a time into the hot oil. Fry to a golden brown, about 3 minutes. Remove pork and drain on a paper towel. Let oil cool and remove from the pan carefully saving 3 tablespoons for stir-frying.

Insert slicing blade. Cut pepper in half and cut rounded edges off the top and bottom, slice. Hand cut the tomato into 8 pieces.

Insert plastic blade. Combine sauce ingredients.

Heat three tablespoons of oil in wok and stir-fry green pepper for 30 seconds. Add pineapple and tomatoes, stir for additional 15 seconds. Add the pork, stir to combine, add sauce and stir-fry until sauce thickens. Serve hot with rice.

Makes 4 servings.

Chicken with Lichee ✓

2 whole chicken breats skinned, boned and
  partially frozen
2 slices ginger root, peeled
3 tablespoons peanut oil
2 tablespoons light soy sauce
2 tablespoons white wine
1/2 cup canned lichees, drained
1/2 cup canned pineapple chunks, drained
1/2 cup canned pineapple juice
2 tablespoons cornstarch

Insert slicing blade. Slice the chicken using heavy pressure. Set aside.

Insert steel blade. With machine running, drop in the ginger and continue processing until finely minced.

Place peanut oil in wok or heavy skillet. When the oil is hot add ginger. Stir-fry until light brown. Add chicken. Stir-fry until chicken is cooked. Add soy sauce and wine and mix well. Add pineapple and lichees and stir.

Add pineapple juice and cornstarch mixture stirring until mixture thickens. Serve with rice, serve hot.

Makes 4 servings.

Mandarin Orange Ice ✓

peel of 1 orange
1 cup sugar
1 cup water
2 cups canned mandarin oranges, drained
1/4 cup lemon juice
orange flavored liqueur, to taste
1 cup canned mandarin oranges, drained (for garnish)

Insert steel blade. Place orange peel and sugar in bowl. Process until peel is chopped. Combine the sugar and orange peel with water in a medium saucepan. Stir until sugar is dissolved. Boil 5 minutes. Remove from heat and cool.

Insert steel blade. Puree mandarin oranges, using ON/OFF motion. Add orange syrup, lemon juice, liqueur and mix well. Put in medium bowl, and place in freezer until firm. Remove.

Insert plastic blade. Process frozen mixture until soft. Pour into 6 individual custard cups or parfait glasses and refreeze. To serve garnish with a few slices of mandarin oranges and mint leaves. Remove from freezer 1/2 hour before serving.

Makes 6 servings.

INDEX

NEED MORE BOOKS?
WANT ONE SENT AS A GIFT?

Yes! Please send me

_____copies of **"INSIDE THE FOOD PROCESSOR"** at $5.00 plus $.75 postage and handling.

_____copies of **"ORIENTAL EXPRESS"** at $5.00 plus $.75 postage and handling.

(N.J. residents add 5% sales tax.)

_____ Total enclosed.

Mail to:

Name _____

Street_____Apt.# _____

City, State & Zip _____

☐ Check here if this is a gift. Card with sender's name will be enclosed.

Please send check or money order to:

GOOD FOOD BOOKS
17 Colonial Terrace
Maplewood, New Jersey 07040

NEED MORE BOOKS?
WANT ONE SENT AS A GIFT?

Yes! Please send me

_____copies of **"INSIDE THE FOOD PROCESSOR"** at $5.00 plus $.75 postage and handling.

_____copies of **"ORIENTAL EXPRESS"** at $5.00 plus $.75 postage and handling.

(N.J. residents add 5% sales tax.)

_____Total enclosed.

Mail to:

Name _____

Street_____Apt.# _____

City, State & Zip _____

☐ Check here if this is a gift. Card with sender's name will be enclosed.

Please send check or money order to:

GOOD FOOD BOOKS
17 Colonial Terrace
Maplewood, New Jersey 07040

NEED MORE BOOKS?
WANT ONE SENT AS A GIFT?

Yes! Please send me

_____copies of **"INSIDE THE FOOD PROCESSOR"** at $5.00 plus $.75 postage and handling.

_____copies of **"ORIENTAL EXPRESS"** at $5.00 plus $.75 postage and handling.

(N.J. residents add 5% sales tax.)

_____Total enclosed.

Mail to:
Name _____

Street_____Apt. # _____

City, State & Zip _____

☐ Check here if this is a gift. Card with sender's name will be enclosed.

Please send check or money order to:

GOOD FOOD BOOKS
17 Colonial Terrace
Maplewood, New Jersey 07040

NEED MORE BOOKS?
WANT ONE SENT AS A GIFT?

Yes! Please send me

_____copies of **"INSIDE THE FOOD PROCESSOR"** at $5.00 plus $.75 postage and handling.

_____copies of **"ORIENTAL EXPRESS"** at $5.00 plus $.75 postage and handling.

(N.J. residents add 5% sales tax.)

_____Total enclosed.

Mail to:
Name _____

Street_____Apt. # _____

City, State & Zip _____

☐ Check here if this is a gift. Card with sender's name will be enclosed.

Please send check or money order to:

GOOD FOOD BOOKS
17 Colonial Terrace
Maplewood, New Jersey 07040